Keys to Online Learning

Keys
TO ONLINE LEARNING

Kateri **Drexler** Carol **Carter** Joyce **Bishop** Sarah **Lyman Kravits**

PEARSON

Boston Columbus Indianapolis New York San Francisco Upper Saddle River
Amsterdam Cape Town Dubai London Madrid Milan Munich Paris Montreal Toronto
Delhi Mexico City Sao Paulo Sydney Hong Kong Seoul Singapore Taipei Tokyo

Editor-in-Chief: Jodi McPherson
Editorial Assistant: Clara Ciminelli
Director of Marketing: Margaret Waples
Executive Marketing Manager: Amy Judd
Production Editor: Gregory Erb
Editorial Production Service: Omegatype Typography, Inc.
Manufacturing Buyer: Megan Cochran
Electronic Composition: Omegatype Typography, Inc.
Interior Design: Omegatype Typography, Inc.
Photo Researcher: Annie Pickert
Cover Administrator: Linda Knowles
Cover Designer: John Wincek

Credits and acknowledgments borrowed from other sources and reproduced, with permission, in this textbook appear on appropriate page within text. All photos © Shutterstock.

Library of Congress Cataloging-in-Publication Data

Keys to online learning / Kateri Drexler . . . [et al.].
        p.   cm.
  Includes bibliographical references and index.
  ISBN-13: 978-0-13-248459-6 (pbk.)
  ISBN-10: 0-13-248459-5 (pbk.)
  1. Educational technology—United States.   2. Web-based instruction.   3. Educational technology—United States.   4. Web-based instruction.   I. Drexler, Kateri M.   II. Title.
  LB1028.3.K49 2012
  371.33'44678   dc22

                                                                    2010041659

10 9 8 7 6 5 4 3 2 1   RRD-OH   15 14 13 12 11

www.pearsonhighered.com

ISBN-10: 0-13-248459-5
ISBN-13: 978-0-13-248459-6

About the Authors

KATERI DREXLER has been designing online applications for students for over fifteen years. As the President of Global Learning Solutions, Inc., Kateri oversees the creation of interactive and engaging online courses, labs, and simulations. Prior to venturing into the online world, she was a professor of business administration and has authored or co-authored twelve texts in the field of student success.

Kateri is dedicated to discovering what drives and enables students to learn. When a high school biology teacher challenged her to raise her own standards significantly beyond what she thought possible, it changed the course of her future. Since then, she has studied how others can benefit from finding their own driving force and mastering learning skills by making small adjustments in habits and practices. She has traveled extensively around the world, living and working in Africa, Asia, South America, and the United States, helping thousands of students take control of the factors and forces that shape their lives.

CAROL CARTER began college knowing she was "behind the 8-ball" in terms of her skills. What she lacked in experience, she made up for with elbow grease and persistence. The work paid off and she graduated college with honors and a desire to help other students. Carol's company, LifeBound, is her classroom. Each year, she works with ten to fifteen student interns and graduates who help her develop ideas which, in turn, help students in colleges and school districts around the country. As President of LifeBound, she teaches study, interpersonal, and career skills to middle school and high school students to help them become competitive in today's global world and to create better prepared freshmen entering college. She also trains and teaches faculty in Academic Coaching. Learn more at www.lifebound.com or follow Carol on Twitter.

Her first book, *Majoring in the Rest of Your Life,* launched her writing career and opened the door to her work on the *Keys to Success* series. Her blog site is www.caroljcarter.com.

JOYCE BISHOP has taught college students for more than twenty-two years. After struggling with a learning disability as a student, she went on to earn a PhD in psychology. Right now, she is in her dream job as staff development coordinator at Golden West College, training faculty in learning strategies and online teaching techniques while still teaching three classes. In 2008 Joyce received the Hayward Award, a state teaching award.

Joyce co-founded the Pathways to Independence non-profit foundation for poor young women from abusive backgrounds. While the young women have come from backgrounds as diverse as prison or extreme poverty, the program has sent 255 of them to college and 195 have graduated into gainful employment. This photo is of Joyce with one of the Pathways graduates, Valerie, who obtained her degree in nursing and is now working at a major university hospital.

SARAH LYMAN KRAVITS lives the strategies for success she writes about. As an author and mother of three children aged 11, 9, and 5, she faces the challenges of managing time and fulfilling responsibilities (not to mention eating right and getting enough sleep). In her writing and research, she works to stay creative and keep up with technology and the growth of knowledge. In her work with colleagues all over the country, she strives for integrity, effective communication, productive teamwork, and flexibility. Finally, in her current role as a breast cancer patient, she uses goal achievement and stress management strategies every single day to get through a host of new and unexpected challenges.

Contents

Chapter 1

Logging In to Success   1

chapter 2

Managing Time and Priorities   16

chapter 3

Navigating Learning Strategies   32

chapter 4
Critical Thinking: Programming   50

chapter 5

Online Reading, Information Literacy, and Study Skills: Uploading Information 66

chapter 6

Note-Taking for Online Courses: Compressing Information 82

chapter 7

Online Course Assignments and Test-Taking: Zooming In 96

chapter 8
Creating e-Portfolios   114

Preface

Online education is creating exciting opportunities for many students. By offering the convenience that traditional courses do not, greater numbers of students can access degree programs, sometimes completing them in an accelerated fashion. However, learning online presents different challenges than found in traditional learning. This text is for anyone preparing for or taking an online course, enrolled in an online program, or using online technology as a supplement to a traditional on-campus course in a blended environment.

Online education has changed how learning occurs. Through new technologies that these courses can offer, in the form of interactive experiences, integrated media, and new communication forms not available in the traditional setting, you can experience far richer and more impactful learning than in a traditional course. Instruction unfolds in a different manner as well. In onsite courses, information is often presented to all students at the same pace within a planned structure. Basic concepts are introduced first, with more complex knowledge revealed as the course progresses. In online courses you decide how and when you access the materials. You will have more freedom, but the skills you need to be successful will likely be very different.

This book provides you with a "how to" approach for navigating online courses. Though some study skill practices that have proven successful in the traditional classroom can, and should, be applied to an online environment, this text presents new strategies that are appropriate for the online setting. An online course requires different techniques for reading, for instance, which often occurs mainly onscreen. Moreover, writing is the main form of communication, and you will need to be able to communicate effectively informally, such as on discussion boards, while also learning formal writing skills required in academic papers. Many instructors find that students also have trouble applying critical thinking skills in the online environment, so a specific chapter in this text is dedicated to enhancing those skills. Because assignments in online courses often require virtual collaboration with other students, the text discusses how the development of virtual professional relationships requires a different set of skills than those used in face-to-face settings. Additionally, the nature of online education can also make a student more anonymous, so we discuss how successful online students need to learn techniques of self-motivation.

Keys to Online Learning Helps You Learn

Focus on Study Skills

Any student taking an online course in any discipline or enrolled in an online or blended program will find this book indispensable. Study skills are covered to a great extent, focused on very specific strategies that online learners can implement for each of a variety of study skills.

Learning Focus Throughout the Text

Once learning styles are introduced and explained in detail in Chapter 3, students are able to assess themselves. Throughout the rest of the text, specific strategies for online learners targeted toward each learning style are highlighted for various situations.

Critical Thinking

The entire chapter devoted to critical thinking is especially important for online students, whose courses offer many opportunities for arguments and analyses in online discussions and assignments. Chapter 4 addresses the importance of using critical thinking while reading, writing, participating in discussions, and completing other assignments for online courses.

Keys to Online Learning Helps You Grow

Self-Assessments in Each Chapter

Each chapter has an assessment at the beginning and an interpretation of the score. This helps set the stage for the material to come and relates it to the student's own life.

Online Outlook

Each chapter includes one or more interview snippets from online students. These Online Outlooks showcase students who have overcome significant challenges to achieve success in online courses or programs.

Keys to Online Learning Helps You Develop Analytical, Creative, and Practical Thinking Skills

Analyze, Create, Practice

Each chapter begins with a question designed to assess, analyze, compare, or evaluate information pertinent to online learning. Creative exercises within each chapter are structured to shift perspectives so students can think outside the box while absorbing the important information.

End of Chapter Exercises

Each Practice exercise is broken into two stages: Plan and Apply. These exercises encourage the synthesis of knowledge presented in the chapter to promote development of a skill set necessary to compete in a knowledge economy.

Additionally, most chapters contain an Online Application exercise that helps you take what you have learned in the chapter and apply it immediately to your online education.

Chapter Highlights

- **Chapter 1.** This chapter focuses on the practices and habits of successful online learners and includes information about the structures and resources common in online education, as well as general advice on setting yourself up for success in your classes.

- **Chapter 2.** Online students face greater challenges with electronic intrusions on time. This chapter addresses how to manage your time and set goals in an online environment, including e-mail, class discussions, assignments, social networking sites, and more. Steps for creating a schedule, including the use of an electronic calendar option, are presented.

- **Chapter 3.** Self-assessments for two different learning styles, along with detailed explanations and strategies, are introduced. Specific suggestions for approaching online courses in general are offered for each learning style.

- **Chapter 4.** The discussion of critical thinking describes how to take apart an issue or argument and find its conclusion, premises, and assumptions. Specific suggestions for online courses include strategies for engaging in discussions, researching information, and using information to solve problems.

- **Chapter 5.** Reading online and in print are very different. Both online and general reading methodologies are presented and explained. Strategies for reducing eyestrain and using learning style strengths for reading are also included.

- **Chapter 6.** There are a number of tools for note-taking from online sources. Strategies for where to keep notes, how to take notes from multimedia sources, using others' notes (or not), and collaborative note-taking skills are presented in this chapter, ending with specific strategies for note-taking that capitalize on learning style strengths.

- **Chapter 7.** Almost all communication that occurs in an online course is through writing. Because of this, writing challenges experienced by many students, regardless of environment, particularly affect online students. Though many similarities exist between writing in an onsite and online environment, this chapter focuses on the challenges of, and strategies for, writing online assignments. For example, the consistent use of informal language, the prevalence of online reading material that makes copying and pasting easy, and the ability to rely on an online community for support create a different experience for online students in terms of their approach to academic writing.

- **Chapter 8.** After learning many skills throughout this text that are applicable and necessary for your career success, Chapter 8 helps you identify and present your unique skills and abilities through an electronic portfolio. You will learn what to include, how to navigate the common e-portfolio platforms, and how to best showcase your talents and knowledge gained through your education and other activities.

Acknowledgments

We knew that introducing a student success textbook for a new and growing market of online learners would generate excitement. In a new endeavor, there are also many unknown factors and different directions to take. Fortunately, we had some fearless advisors who were anxious to share their knowledge with future students to better prepare them for a new learning experience. We would like to thank all those who contributed ideas and feedback in our early planning stages, including Sunand Bhattacharya, Dr. Jane Drexler, Charlotte Morrissey, and Chelsey Emmelhainz. We would also like to especially thank our editor, Sande Johnson, whose input, guidance, and devotion to student success across the curricula has driven the development of this text and has enabled us to offer a comprehensive guide for online learners as rapidly as possible. We are immensely grateful for the time, energy, and thought that our advisors generously gave.

We would also like to thank our excellent team of reviewers who offered extensive feedback, including Laurie Adamson, Olympic College; Mark Brasher, ITT Technical Institute; Jeremy Dunning, Indiana University; Diane Eisenberg, Chapman University; Robyn Greenberg, North Carolina A&T University; William Shultz, Walden University; Lisa Taylor-Galizia, Carteret Community College; and Kimberly Toby, Somerset Community College.

Finally, we thank Nancy Forsyth, President of the Teacher Education Group at Pearson, and Jodi McPherson, Editor-in-Chief for Student Success and Career Development, for their support and vision.

For Students!

Why is this course important?

This course will help you transition to college, introduce you to campus resources, and prepare you for success in all aspects of college, career, and life. You will:
- Develop Skills to Excel in Other Classes
- Apply Concepts from College to Your Career and Life
- Learn to Use Media Resources

How can you get the most out of the book and online resources required in this class?

Purchase your book and online resources before the First Day of Class. Register and log in to the online resources using your access code.

Develop Skills to Excel in Other Classes
- Helps you with your homework
- Prepares you for exams

Apply Concepts from College to Your Career and Life
- Provides learning techniques
- Helps you achieve your goals

Learn to Use Media Resources
- **www.mystudentsuccesslab.com** helps you build skills you need to succeed through peer-led videos, interactive exercises and projects, journaling and goal setting activities.
- Connect with real students, practice skill development, and personalize what is learned.

Want to get involved with Pearson like other students have?

Join www.PearsonStudents.com

It is a place where our student customers can incorporate their views and ideas into their learning experience. They come to find out about our programs such as the **Pearson Student Advisory Board**, **Pearson Campus Ambassador**, and the **Pearson Prize** (student scholarship!).

Here's how you can get involved:

- Tell your instructors, friends, and family members about **PearsonStudents**.
- To get daily updates on how students can boost their resumes, study tips, get involved with Pearson, and earn rewards:

   Become a fan of **Pearson Students on Facebook**

   Follow **@Pearson_Student on Twitter**

- Explore **Pearson Free Agent**. It allows you get involved in the publishing process, by giving student feedback.

See you on **PearsonStudents** where our student customers live. When students succeed, we succeed!

PEARSON
mystudentsuccesslab

Succeed in college and beyond!
Connect, practice, and personalize with MyStudentSuccessLab.

www.mystudentsuccesslab.com

MyStudentSuccessLab is an online solution designed to help students acquire the skills they need to succeed. They will have access to peer-led video presentations and develop core skills through interactive exercises and projects that provide academic, life, and career skills that will transfer to ANY course.

It can accompany any Student Success text, or be sold as a stand-alone course offering. To become successful learners, students must consistently apply techniques to daily activities.

How will MyStudentSuccessLab make a difference?

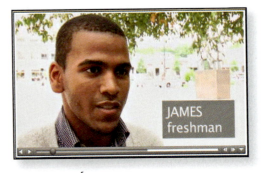

Is motivation a challenge, and if so, how do you deal with it?
Video Presentation — Experience peer led video 'by students, for students' of all ages and stages.

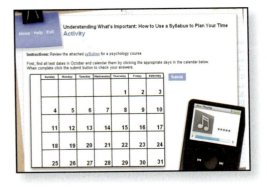

How would better class preparation improve the learning experience?
Practice activities — Practice skills for each topic — beginning, intermediate, and advanced — leveled by Bloom's taxonomy.

Now Available!
A 'one-stop shop' for student success.

This website offers a compilation of Pearson's training, resources, and support options all in one convenient place.

We provide variety of **Training** options to meet your needs. Events and Workshops around the country as well as Online Webinars. MyStudentSuccessLab Technology training is available too.

A wealth of **Resources** are available to address a range of interests, including assessments, online catalog, customized solutions, Instructor Resources, and Student Resources. Technology is addressed, whether you're teaching online, hybrid, or just need an engagement tool.

For **Support**, always contact your local sales professional, however, the SSCD Team is here to help anytime including Customer Service, Technical Support, Editorial, Events, Marketing, Specialists, and Faculty Advocates.

Welcome to the **Pearson SSCD Online Community** where we connect, empower, and renew with one another. Regardless of your institute origin, teaching background, or experience level, we strive to ensure there are resources available to support our mission—infusing success for EVERY student and instructor!

www.pearsonhighered.com/sscd4success

Keys to Online Learning

LOGGING IN
to Success

UNDERSTANDING THE ONLINE LEARNING ENVIRONMENT

- Facts and Fictions of Online Learning
- Types of Online Courses
- Types of Assignments
- Types of Learning Management Systems

SETTING YOURSELF UP FOR SUCCESS: PRACTICES OF SUCCESSFUL ONLINE LEARNERS

- Prepare for the Path Ahead
- Structure Your Schedule
- Set Priorities
- Develop Discipline and Accountability
- Foster Relationships
- Seek New Skills
- Manage Your Thoughts and Emotions
- Ask for Help

ASK YOURSELF

What do you want out of this course—and out of your college education? What are you willing to do to make sure that you get it?

IN THIS CHAPTER

you'll explore answers to the following questions:

- What are some of the benefits and challenges of online learning?
- What can I expect to find in an online course?
- What practices are important for succeeding in online courses?

Analyze

Taking a self-assessment can help you think more deeply about your own skills and preferences. Consider the questions in this assessment and your responses. What information does this quiz give you about yourself that you can use to develop or improve important skills?

Rate Yourself as an Online Student

For each statement, circle the number that feels right to you, from 1 for "not true for me" to 5 for "very true for me."

▶ I feel prepared to handle online college-level work.	1 2 3 4 5
▶ I understand how online courses differ from offerings in traditional classrooms.	1 2 3 4 5
▶ I feel comfortable communicating in writing.	1 2 3 4 5
▶ I try to find a way to connect new information with what I already know.	1 2 3 4 5
▶ When I learn information or a skill, I consider how it may help me in the future.	1 2 3 4 5
▶ I refer to the syllabus for each of my courses frequently.	1 2 3 4 5
▶ I understand the skills that I will gain from each course in my program and how these will benefit me in my future career.	1 2 3 4 5
▶ I am comfortable using the college's learning management system (LMS).	1 2 3 4 5
▶ When I need help, I find—and reach out to—the resources my college provides.	1 2 3 4 5
▶ I relate effectively to others and can work successfully in a virtual team.	1 2 3 4 5

Now total your scores.   _____

If your total ranges from 38–50, you consider yourself ready to actively engage in your online program. You understand why your course is important to your future success. You are a self-starter who takes responsibility for getting things done, and you feel relatively comfortable writing, which is an often-used skill in online courses.

If your total ranges from 24–37, you consider your online college readiness to be average. A couple of minor adjustments in your expectations, and you should be on your way. When online students understand why a course is important to their future success, it provides motivation during the more difficult times. Make sure you take responsibility for getting things done and learn more about how to motivate yourself, if you need that skill. If you do not feel relatively comfortable writing your thoughts, remember that practice makes perfect. Overcome your fear, and begin. Most of the communication you do in an online course is in writing.

If your total ranges from 10–23, you think you need some additional skills to face the challenges of an online education. Determine why a particular course is important to your future success. Your success is in your hands—and yours alone. Take responsibility for getting work done. You can learn more about how to motivate yourself in this chapter. Because you will be on your own much of the time in an online learning environment, you will need to make yourself take the necessary action. Most of the communication you do in an online course is in writing. If you do not feel comfortable writing, use techniques presented in this course to overcome your fear so you can actively participate.

Analyze: What skills are important for an online course? What skills do you want to develop or improve? How is education online different from that in a traditional classroom? How is it the same?

Taking online courses has a cost—
in time, money, and energy.

By signing up for an online course, you have entered an exciting realm of learning. You are joining a group of over 4.6 million college students who are taking advantage of the convenience and opportunities that online education offers. In fact, online enrollments are growing at a faster rate than traditional course enrollments. Today, more than one in four college students are taking at least one online course.[†]

Benefits of Online Learning

- *Flexible scheduling.* Online students can focus on what they need to learn when they choose. You can access the content you need when you need it.

- *High-quality interaction.* Online students often have *more* interaction and enhanced relationships than in a traditional classroom. You have time to think and process information before responding to others. The virtual collaboration skills you gain by working in groups are highly valued in the workplace.

- *Interactive and engaging media.* Through new technologies that online courses can offer, including new communication methods, interactivity, animations, videos, and audio podcasts, you can learn complex concepts in a variety of ways.

- *Technological comfort level.* Graduates from online programs learn to become proactive users of technology.

Though online courses offer a number of resources to enhance your learning experience and help prepare you for a successful career, they also pose unique challenges. The skills required for successful learning in an online environment are different from those needed in a traditional classroom. For instance, developing virtual peer relationships demands a different approach than building team skills in a face-to-face environment. Reading onscreen differs from reading a textbook. And because writing is the main form of communication in an online course, you will need to be able to communicate effectively in writing both formally, for written assignments, and less formally, for written discussions and e-mails.

The most important skill you can have in an online class is the ability to take charge of your own learning. Instead of receiving the same instruction at the same pace within a planned structure as those in a traditional course, online students often have to make decisions about how and when to access course materials. Will you look at the course resources first, jump to the weblinks offered, or go to the assignments immediately? The nature of online education can also make you more anonymous. If you never log in, a class could end without anyone calling or e-mailing to find out where your assignments are. **Successful online students tend to be self-starters and highly motivated to complete assignments and do well in these courses.**

The U.S. Department of Education analyzed research studies undertaken from 1996 to 2008 and has concluded that online education is more effective than face-to-face learning.[*]

---

[*]U.S. Department of Education. (2009, May). *Evaluation of Evidence-Based Practices in Online Learning: A Meta-Analysis and Review of Online Learning Studies.* Retrieved March 2, 2010, from www.geteducated.com/images/pdfs/doe_online_education_finalreport.pdf

[†]Allen, E., & Seaman, J. (2010). *Learning on Demand: Online Education in the United States, 2009.* Newburyport, MA: The Sloan Consortium and Babson Survey Research Group.

You Have Much to Gain from College

Studies by the U.S. Department of Education show the gains that college graduates are likely to make:

- *Increased income.* College graduates earn, on average, around $20,000 more per year than those with only a high school diploma.
- *Increased chances of finding and keeping a job.* The unemployment rate for college graduates is less than half that of high school graduates.
- *Better health.* With the knowledge and increased self-awareness that college often brings, both college graduates and their children are more likely to stay healthy.
- *More money for the future.* College graduates, on average, put away more money in savings.
- *Broader thinking.* College graduates tend to be more open-minded and less prejudiced. They also generally have more understanding of different cultures and more knowledge of what's going on in the world.
- *Better decision making.* As consumers, college graduates tend to think more critically and comprehensively about the pros and cons before making a purchase.

Understanding
the Online Learning Environment

It is helpful to start your online course or program by knowing as much as you can about what to expect. Though you may have some ideas about how online learning works, there may be aspects that you have not considered. Start by assessing some of the facts and fictions of learning online.

Facts and Fictions of Online Learning

Fact or Fiction?

Online courses can be impersonal, disconnected, and unfulfilling.

Fiction. Although online courses are set up differently than onsite courses, there is just as much opportunity for interaction once you get used to communicating through cyberspace. Much of the time, in fact, students find that they are more self-revealing and their discussions get deeper than they do in an onsite classroom. In many ways, online courses create a more level playing field where the focus is solely on content and the learning process. You will not need to worry about appearance, age, disability, race, or even your wardrobe. You may be surprised by the rewarding experiences you find in the online classroom environment.

Fact or Fiction?

Online classes are easier than onsite classes.

Fiction. Both traditional and online classes will differ in terms of their requirements, the instructor's methods, and your initial level of understanding. However, online courses are *not* easier. In fact, they can be more difficult than an onsite class. For instance, a typical online course is shorter in duration but still requires the same amount of work as its onsite counterpart. In most online courses, there is also a lot of additional writing, which some students find more challenging.

Fact or Fiction?

Online instructors are less attentive than onsite instructors.

Fiction. Instructors, whether onsite or online, differ in their approach, and their levels of engagement can depend on many factors. However, most online instructors do spend a great deal of time engaging the class. They shoulder a larger burden because they don't have the benefit of nonverbal cues available to an onsite instructor, such as body language or bored yawns. Your instructor's level of engagement, however, is out of your control. **If you find you need additional help to stay engaged, ask your instructor immediately.**

Fact or Fiction?

Online courses are more expensive than onsite courses.

Fiction. When schools first developed online courses, they were more expensive than they are today. With improvements in technology and the standardization of course development, online courses are competitive and sometimes less expensive than onsite courses. Depending on the school, though, an online course may be more expensive initially. After factoring in transportation, fees, child care, parking, and the time it takes to travel back and forth, you may find that the online course is actually less expensive.

Fact or Fiction?

Online courses fit better into a busier schedule.

Fact. As an online student, you can often participate in the instruction at times that are convenient for you. You can attend class in the morning before going to work, during your lunch hour, after you have put the kids to bed, or any other time during your day. You will still have a lot of work to do, but it will be at a time that you have selected.

Besides the convenience, this flexibility offers additional benefits. Because you save the time you would have spent traveling to class, you can spend more time on learning. You can also focus on learning what you need to know versus sitting through a lecture that may not address your most significant needs.

Fact or Fiction?

You can participate in an online class from anywhere.

Fiction. Though distance learning is often called "anywhere, anytime learning," in practice, you may find this not to be the case. Depending on how you best learn and work, you may need to have resources around you and a dedicated amount of time to work on the assignments. There will be times when you need high-speed Internet to get the full advantage of your online courses. There may be videos, audio recordings, and online texts to access and Internet research to conduct. Online courses are demanding, so you will need to have the proper mindset as well to tackle the challenges. You may find that your concentration is best in certain locations or at certain times. To get the most out of your program, approach these courses with intensity and focus and choose the best working environment.

Fact or Fiction?

Education standards are lower for online courses.

Fiction. Online courses have to be accredited by the same bodies that approve on-site courses. Examined by many authorities, accredited online courses are rigorous and soundly structured, with high standards. They are often developed by the best instructors and use the same curriculum as their onsite counterparts.

Types of Online Courses

Online courses are not all alike. Classes may be fully online or the online portion may combine with a traditional classroom, or onsite, portion, making what is termed a *blended* course. The online portions of blended courses can vary greatly among different offerings, from large to small percentages or anywhere in between.

Most fully online courses are *asynchronous,* meaning that you can access them at your convenience. Some are *synchronous,* however, with set meeting times when everyone will be online at the same time. Some courses use a combination of synchronous and asynchronous modes.

Online courses can take different approaches to providing content in the methods of presentation, materials used, and types of resources offered.

- *Course presentations.* Some online courses will offer textual explanations of the material organized by week or unit, with separately accessed resources. Others might use an integrated course presentation leading the user through the material in a series of screens, with resources such as videos or interactive exercises incorporated into the presentation. Some other courses will simply direct students to access specific information on their own. Pay special attention to material that is within a course presentation—it is usually the most important information.

- *Textbooks and other hard copy materials.* Your textbook may be a printed version, an online document accessed through an e-reader program, or a file (such as a .pdf or Microsoft Word document) that can be downloaded and either printed or read onscreen. Your text is usually one of the most important resources for any course.

- *Video lectures.* Some online courses include video lectures by an instructor, created specifically for the course or taped from previous presentations.

- *Animations and interactive media.* Because of the effort and cost involved in creating animations or interactive media, they are likely centered around the most important concepts in the course. Any interactive media that your course includes is probably worth accessing.

Access your online course and find the following resources:

- Announcements
- Discussion boards
- Course content
- Assignments and assessments
- Gradebook
- Chat room or lounge
- Dropbox/document sharing

What other resources are available in your course? Skim through one lesson. How is the content presented? Where are the assignments found? Next, skim through another lesson and the assignments. Is it set up in the same way as the first? Find your course objectives and the syllabus and determine how you will be graded. If you cannot find an answer to a question, immediately contact your instructor or a support person at your school to find the information.

- *Podcasts.* Users can subscribe to and automatically download new *podcasts*—audio and video programs published via the Internet. Podcasting in online courses might offer full, unabridged audio recordings of the online presentation. Other courses use podcasts that supplement the online portion with instructional explanations, guest speakers, commentaries on current issues, and integration of news media. If your course uses podcasts to supplement the course material, be sure to access them.

- *Weblinks.* Your course might also provide additional weblinks added by the instructor that lead to external websites, videos, and other resources. If you see weblinks listed or any other supplements specifically added by your instructor, these are likely important resources.

Types of Assignments

Within any online course, you might find a mix of any or all of the following:

- *Graded discussions.* One of the most exciting features of an online course is the discussion forum. An instructor posts a question on the threaded (asynchronous) discussion board. Typically, every student in the class is expected to respond intelligently several times to different people. No one is allowed to sit at the back of the class and refrain from participating. **Discussions are the most "visibility" you will have in the class.**

- *Quizzes and exams.* In an online course, quizzes and exams are usually substantially different from traditional tests in that many are open book tests, taken at your convenience within a set time period. Those who experience test anxiety in public will likely be less affected by online tests.

- *Ungraded self-assessments.* Some courses offer pre- and post-assessments to help direct your attention to key course concepts. Take the nongraded practice quizzes and assessments that are built into the course to receive valuable feedback and additional motivation to learn the material.

- *Short written assignments.* Individual written exercises are generally graded multi-part problems or short responses that assess your understanding of the material.

- *Longer analysis papers.* These papers are generally several pages long and may require some type of analysis, such as determining cause-and-effect relationships or persuasive writing attempting to convince readers of a particular point of view.

- *Group projects.* Online courses often feature group projects, which can vary in several significant ways. They can be large and ongoing throughout the term or small assignments taking only a week or two. You may select your group or the instructor may assign you to one. Communication within the group may be public, for everyone to see, or private, for group members only. Sometimes the group is given one grade, and sometimes your grade will be a combination of the group grade and an individual assessment based on peer reviews.

- *Journals.* In some courses journaling is encouraged as a means to reflect on what you are learning and how it relates to your previous knowledge or to some element of your life.

Focus on the key information in the course content. First, look at the unit or lesson objectives before looking at the material. Take a minute to put yourself in the shoes of the course creator. How would you make sure a student learned important information? As you go through the course material, judge the importance and significance of concepts by comparing them to the lesson objectives.

Types of Learning Management Systems

How will you see the content that has been created for an online course? It is usually delivered through what is called a *learning management system* (LMS), which is simply a software program through which a school presents the information and tracks the progress of students. Popular examples include eCollege, Blackboard, Moodle,

Go through the tutorial offered by the school to introduce your program. Read all materials provided.

If you have any trouble understanding the system, get help NOW! Do not wait to ask questions. Call the academic support number or contact your instructor as soon as possible.

Get your course access instructions the week before the course begins. Go through the elements of the LMS and make sure you know how to access and post assignments and discussion responses.

Access a course presentation and download all required multimedia software. Make sure you can view all multimedia files, like videos or interactive presentations.

Keep your passwords, usernames, and tech support numbers where you can readily find them.

Joomla, and Desire2Learn. Your school may use one of these or a proprietary LMS designed specifically for your institution.

Learn to use your LMS as soon as you sign up for your first course. Although differing from each other in some respects, LMSs usually have the following sections:

- Announcements
- Discussion Boards
- Course Content
- Assignments and Assessments
- Gradebook
- Chat Room or Lounge
- Dropbox/DocSharing
- Resources

Instructions to access and navigate the LMS may be found in an online user manual that will usually be provided to you. Make sure that you explore and play around with the course site before your class starts so you know where to find everything and how to post assignments, discussion responses, and other course resources.

You may also be required to access software to view multimedia content by downloading or upgrading to the latest versions of software programs such as the following:

- Quicktime Player
- Adobe FlashPlayer
- Adobe Reader
- Real Player

If your LMS requires you to use any of these, there should be a link to the free download page for each.

If your course has an electronic library resource, you may be able to link to it through the LMS. Make sure you access it and look around at the different resources available. Electronic libraries provide connections to databases that may include full-text online books, full-text magazines and journals, encyclopedias, dictionaries, and more. They may also provide traditional library services in the online environment, such as reference help and curriculum-specific research guides, tutorials, and collections of frequently asked questions and answers. If your course offers such a resource, become familiar with it before you begin your course.

Additional strategies to make the most of your LMS can be found in Key 1.1.

Setting Yourself Up for Success: Practices of Successful Online Learners

You can set yourself up for success in your online course by learning habits that outstanding online students regularly practice (Key 1.2).

1. Prepare for the path ahead
2. Structure your schedule
3. Set priorities
4. Develop discipline and accountability
5. Foster relationships
6. Seek new skills
7. Manage your thoughts and emotions
8. Ask for help

Prepare for the Path Ahead	Structure Your Schedule	Set Priorities	Develop Discipline and Accountability
Good plans shape good decisions. Decide what you want and map out exactly how you're going to get there.	Managing everything you need to do requires a good up-to-date schedule that incorporates due dates for your class, work appointments, and personal commitments.	Keeping your "eye on the prize" can help during the daily grind when multiple demands can seem hard to manage.	The online learning process is normally accelerated and requires commitment. Staying up with the class and completing all work on time is very important.

Foster Relationships	Seek New Skills	Manage Your Thoughts and Emotions	Ask for Help
Being part of a community of learners and establishing a bond or common ground with classmates may mean the difference between a successful, supportive experience and feeling lost and detached.	You may face challenges in developing a new set of skills for a new type of instruction. Determine through this text what is necessary for you and set out to develop those skills.	Your mind can make a huge difference. Trade in negative thoughts for positive ones and become aware of negative emotions.	Surround yourself with motivating and encouraging people. It helps your efforts when you know how to ask for and get the help you need.

Prepare for the Path Ahead

The course catalog is one of your most important resources. Not only does it give you information on school procedures and policies—registration, requirements for majors, transferring, and so on—it also provides a roadmap for your program. How many courses are included? What order are they in? Your catalog also tells you how the current courses you are taking fit into the big picture. Every course in your curriculum has been chosen because it is important to your future career success. Try to determine some of the skills that each course will help you develop and how the overall skill set you will have at the end of the program will help foster success in your career.

Another important resource is your course syllabus, which tells you everything you need to know about your course—when to read chapters and materials, dates of exams and due dates for assignments, how your final grade is calculated, and more. Refer to the syllabus for each course you take throughout the term.

Understanding where you are going will give you motivation and determination to make it through each of the steps required in a class or program. The following strategies can help you prepare for the path ahead:

- Write down your main goal for achieving your education. Keep this in a place where you can see it every day.
- Make a list of all the courses in your program. After you read your course catalog identify one or two important skills you will learn from each course.
- Map out your program—when you will take each course.

Structure Your Schedule

Effective goal setting and smart planning are important tools to have for your online journey. Most goals can be broken down into specific "mini" goals that can be incorporated into a daily schedule.

Logging in to your course every day and checking for new postings or updates can help prevent falling behind.

Make use of your syllabus by putting key dates in your calendar program, spotting time crunches, and getting a sense of how much time you need to set aside to study. Keep a "to-do" list near your schedule and get an idea, at least, of when you will do the important items.

Other strategies to help structure your schedule include the following:

- *Use a calendar.* Schedule standard times in your calendar for studying. Some students find that scheduling study time daily is helpful whereas others choose specific study days in the week. Pick a schedule that can work for you and stick to it.

- *Participate in your course as much as possible.* Check the discussion boards several times throughout the week. If you're required to respond to several posts, you'll get much more out of the course if you do so earlier and then check in later to see what other students have said.

- *Take care of yourself.* You will have to devote a lot of time to your online program, especially initially. Though you may not have a lot of extra time now, taking care of yourself is very important. Make time to do things that help you feel replenished.

Set Priorities

Knowing what you want will help you make time for your goals.

Establish priorities for your life. Then you can be effective at your studies and take care of everyone and everything else in your life. You've chosen to pursue online education for a reason. Most likely, it fits in with one of your major life goals.

Use the following strategies to help set priorities:

- *Understand what you value in life.* How is your education important to your life goals?

- *Make the course a priority.* Logging in to your course and making time for schoolwork should take precedence over other activities. Do and say whatever you have to in order to let family and co-workers know that time for your program is not negotiable.

- *Read success stories.* Find out about others who have achieved the goals you have set for yourself.

- *Think about the effects of your success.* Remind yourself often of what your success will mean to others—those you know and care about already and those current strangers who you are yet to inspire.

Develop Discipline and Accountability

Even with the best of schedules and calendars in place, what matters most is whether you get the work done.

One of the biggest challenges facing an online student is gaining the self-discipline required to be successful. **There is perhaps no single greater habit for online success than becoming a self-starter and managing yourself.** You have to discipline yourself in maintaining your schedule and not allow any distractions to disrupt your plan.

Use the following strategies to help develop discipline and accountability:

- *Keep the pressure down.* Be careful not to put too much pressure on yourself to complete a homework assignment. Leave some time to avoid doing it all at once and to let the concepts "gel" before tackling the project.

- *Find someone to help keep you accountable.* If you are supposed to get something done, it helps to have someone to tell after accomplishing your goal. Your support person may be a classmate who can also inspire and help energize you with ideas providing that needed spark to get started on a project or assignment.

- *Implement the "10-minute" rule.* If you are really stuck on something and cannot find the motivation to even begin, make yourself do something related to the assignment for only 10 minutes, even if it is simply organizing your materials.

- *Remember that this is a marathon and not a sprint.* Long distance runners sometimes find themselves imagining crossing the finish line miles ahead of time. When they come back to reality and realize they aren't anywhere near the end, they can become disheartened. One strategy for runners projecting too far into the future is bringing themselves back to the present with self-talk: "Here I am at mile 8." This gets them back on track emotionally for the run. You can do the same thing. When you find yourself projecting too far ahead, know that the finish line is ahead, but bring yourself back to your present location in the journey.

Foster Relationships

To effectively work in a distance learning environment, you need to feel close to your classmates and instructors, despite the miles that may be between you. Not only does learning increase with social interaction, the meaningful connections you make with your online classmates can translate into friendships and career networking opportunities later.

Communicating online is a bit different from communicating in person. Without the benefit of tone, body language, or social cues like proximity or volume, it becomes much more important to stay positive, remain tolerant and polite, and eliminate language that could be easily misinterpreted.

Other strategies to help foster relationships online include the following:

- *Interact with the other students as much as possible.* In the discussion forum, add something meaningful by posting a response, question, or comment to several other students' postings. Interact with as many students as possible to build online relationships.

- *Value diversity.* You may interact with people from many different backgrounds and cultures in an online course. As you build your knowledge about other cultures and appreciate and accept the differences, you heighten your ability to analyze how people relate to one another. Most important, you develop practical skills that enable you to bridge the gap between yourself and others. Gain as much information as you can by reading about different cultures. Strive to treat others with tolerance and respect, avoiding assumptions and granting them the right to think and believe without being judged.

- *Ask questions.* Seek out people you might not ordinarily get a chance to befriend. Ask about their lives and traditions.

- *Prioritize personal relationships.* When you devote time and energy to education, work, and activities you enjoy, you get positive results. Do the same for your relationships. If you treat others with the kind of loyalty and support that you appreciate, you are likely to receive the same in return.

- *Check in with people based on their past posts.* If someone mentioned a problem earlier, ask about it this week. This is a great way to make your classmates feel valued.

- *Be open minded.* Share life, work, and educational experiences as part of the learning process. Telling personal stories makes the material relevant, and revealing something about your life lets classmates know you better.

- *Work through tensions, if possible.* Negative feelings can grow and cause problems when left unspoken. Try to resolve the problems if you can. However, know that sometimes relationships fail regardless of what you do. When an important relationship becomes strained or breaks up, analyze the situation and choose practical strategies to move on. Some people need time alone; others need to be with friends and family. Some need a change of scene; others need to let off steam with exercise or other activities. Whatever you do, believe that in time you will emerge from the experience stronger.

Incorporate a plan for regular communication with your classmates into your overall course schedule for greater success in online learning.

RUCHA

Working professional and online student Age 35

CHALLENGE

Mother of three and employed full-time

The major benefit of learning online as opposed to a classroom for me is mainly the ability to go to class anytime I want. Having a full-time job, a family, and doing volunteer work requires a lot of time, and I am able to complete most of my schoolwork some evenings and on the weekend without leaving my house and driving to a campus.

The major challenge is just getting my work finished on time. You must have the willpower to sit down and do your work instead of vegging out in front of the TV. It is very easy to procrastinate.

I force myself to sit down and finish a set amount of work or reach a certain point in my reading before I allow myself to do other things.

It helped me to set a desk area up and time slots that are exclusively dedicated to my schoolwork. I am very disciplined about this.

Since most of the reading can be done away from my desk, I usually do that in a comfortable spot, on the bus, or during a break at work.

Prejudice

To be prejudiced means to prejudge others, usually on the basis of gender, race, sexual orientation, disability, religion, and other characteristics. Prejudice may creep up on you without your even knowing it because of factors like the following:

- *Influence of family and culture.* Children learn attitudes—including intolerance, superiority, and hate—from their parents, peers, and community.
- *Fear of differences.* It is human to fear the unfamiliar and make assumptions about it.
- *Experience.* One bad experience with a person of a particular race or religion may lead someone to condemn all people with the same background.

Stereotypes

Prejudice is usually based on **stereotypes**—assumptions made, without proof or critical thinking, about the characteristics of a person or group. Stereotyping comes from factors such as the following:

- *Desire for patterns and logic.* People often try to make sense of the world by using the labels, categories, and generalizations that stereotypes provide.
- *Media influences.* The more people see stereotypical images, the easier it is to believe that stereotypes are universal.
- *Laziness.* Labeling group members according to a characteristic they seem to have in common takes less energy than asking questions that illuminate the qualities of individuals.

Stereotypes derail personal connections and block effective communication, because pasting a label on a person makes it hard for you to see the real person underneath. Even stereotypes that seem "positive" may not be true and may get in the way of perceiving uniqueness.

Seek New Skills

Most successful online students tend to have a proficiency in certain study skills. They adapt to reading on a screen, taking notes from online material, collaborating with a diverse group of people, navigating the learning management system used in the course, and embracing new concepts.

Consider how you read online, for instance. Jakob Nielsen, a Web researcher, tested how 232 people read pages on monitors.* Using eye-tracking tools to map how vision moves and rests, he found that people read online in a formation that looks like the capital letter "F." At the top, users read all the way across, but as they proceed their descent quickens and horizontal sight contracts, with a slowdown around the middle of the page. Near the bottom, eyes move almost vertically, and the lower-right corner of the page is largely ignored. People read quickly online, too. Though this has advantages for reading a great number of web pages with a lot of content, it might not serve you when reading an online textbook or when needing to understand difficult material. Be aware of your reading patterns and alter them when necessary.

In the online classroom, nearly all communication is written, so it is critical that you feel comfortable expressing yourself in writing.

Collaboration is also a key skill in the online community. You may find yourself learning with people from all over. Being able to communicate and collaborate at a distance is a valuable skill that will help to broaden your horizons.

Find more information about the skills that challenge you and practice them to become a better learner.

Other strategies for seeking out and learning new skills include the following:

- *Apply new material to what you already know.* Relate new concepts to a current or past experience.

- *Practice with the collaborative technologies available.* "Meet" with your classmates, share documents, or brainstorm on a whiteboard in real time together.

- *Put new knowledge to work as soon as possible.* As soon as possible after studying, apply the new knowledge you have learned through collaboration with other classmates, at your place of employment, or in your home.

- *If you are having trouble, contact your instructor immediately.* You can also find academic support to help you. Don't wait! Call them as soon as you don't understand something or have trouble navigating the technology.

Manage Your Thoughts and Emotions

Reaching new levels in your life requires changing from the inside out. Successful online students have found ways of preventing burnout or loss of interest by talking themselves through it.

Emotions can be quite high in distance learning, heightened by the lack of face-to-face interaction. Life, in general, has ups and downs too, with commitments, disappointments, and conflict. Find ways to push past the negative thoughts and emotions that may come up. Think of all the advances you have already made, affirm what you will do and how you will do it, and don't try to do too much too quickly. Develop positive thoughts to replace the negative ones and repeat those positive thoughts as often as possible.

Other strategies to manage your thoughts and emotions include the following:

- *Take action!* If you have fallen behind in a course, do something simple like finishing the assignment, participating in a discussion, or reading the material. Even small, positive actions can set you back on course.

- *Focus on the positives.* Reflect on what you can do, not on what you can't. Think about what you did, not what you didn't, and what you will do instead of what you won't.

- *Face your fears by acknowledging them.* Giving fear a name lessens its hold on you. Dig deeper. Is there something else that you are afraid of that you have not seen? Challenge it using positive self-talk. If it persists, feel the fear and do what you need to do anyway.

Become aware of any negative thoughts you have. Pay attention to: "should," "ought," "have to," "can't," "always," and "never." Challenge those thoughts—is there a real reason or is it just fear that makes you think them?

*Nielsen, J., & Pernice, K. (2009). *Eyetracking Web Usability*. Berkeley, CA: New Riders Press.

Create a Quick Plan for Success

What can you do today that will have the most impact for success in your online program? What can you do tomorrow? Next week? Next month?

• *Learn the lesson and move on.* If you have made mistakes, learn the lessons from them and then erase the feelings by interrupting your standard thought patterns. Interject funny music in the background of your memories or see people as distorted when you find the scene repeating itself in your memory over and over. See the memory in forward and reverse—thinking about anything silly along with the memory can disrupt how you think about past mistakes so you can move on and not let them hold you back.

• *Find the benefits in any situation.* Sometimes you are faced with difficult situations or hard times that you cannot control. First, find the benefit—there is usually something positive in anything. Ask yourself, "What can be good about this?" Perhaps the situation is forcing you to learn a new skill or do something you might not otherwise have had the chance to do. Then ask yourself what is not yet perfect in the situation and what you can do to move it in that direction.

• *Spend time with positive people who care about you.* You need and deserve people in your life who support your efforts.

Ask For Help

> When you do not understand something fully, it is seldom the case that you are alone in your struggle. By asking questions, in fact, you may help other students.

Many students find that they are afraid to ask for help when they don't understand something, whether it is information they learn in a course, general information about their program of study, or specific features of a new technology, such as the learning management system. You are investing significant resources in order to complete your program, and it is your right and your responsibility to find the information you need. Your instructors, deans, academic counselors, and the entire administration are here to help you. They want to be helpful and are waiting for the opportunity. Even if you feel like you should already know the answer, but don't—ask someone!

You can also ask questions of your fellow classmates. Indeed, asking questions is integral to learning.

In addition to receiving help within your course, you may also find that you need to ask for help from your family and friends to make it through your program. When you do so, you are allowing them to contribute to your efforts and success.

Strategies to ask for help include the following:

• *Gather contact information.* Learn how to reach the people who can be resources during your education. Include instructors, administrators, deans, academic counselors, family members, friends, babysitters, and any other potential resources. Keep their phone numbers handy and make it a habit to ask for and incorporate their help as often as possible.

• *Speak clearly.* You deserve the help you need. Identify specifically what you need.

- *Understand that not everybody is willing to help.* Have a plan in place for dealing with the people who may try to stop you from doing what you need to do to succeed.
- *Lean on your classmates.* They understand what you are going through and can offer suggestions and strategies to get the help you need.

PRACTICE & plan apply

The purpose of this exercise is to give you a chance to discover and acknowledge your own strengths and identify areas needing improvement. To make this assignment worthwhile, approach it with courage, understanding that it can allow you to develop your own plan for success in the online school environment.

List at least two practices that successful online students have in common. For instance, you might list the following: Online Learners Take Responsibility for Their Own Learning.

PLAN

Under each practice, identify your skill level in this area by writing a few sentences describing how you have used this skill in the past. For instance, most successful online learners prepare for the path ahead. This means they know what is coming and how each of their courses relates to their overall career goal. Do you know your educational path and why it is set up the way it is? How close is your response to the following example?

1. Online Learners Prepare for the Path Ahead.

I honestly haven't done this yet. I've been so busy trying to work and raise a family that education has been low on my list. I guess I've expected other people to teach me something if they want me to know it, but I haven't assessed why I need certain skills.

Now look at how you evaluated yourself on each trait and suggest at least two ways that you might improve. These suggestions should be action items. For instance, in the responsibility example, you might write something like the following:

I have realized that education is vital to my future, and it is no longer low on my list. I need to start figuring out what I need to do to get to where I want to be. This means that I need to:

- Get my course catalog and map out my program—when I will take each course and what skills I will gain from each.
- Identify the learning objectives of the courses I am taking now.
- Ask my instructor questions immediately if I do not understand how something relates to the learning objectives.

APPLY

Now act on your plan. Give yourself a little time, and come back to this exercise. How is it working out?

MANAGING
Time and Priorities

2

SETTING GOALS FOR SUCCESS

- What Is a Goal?
- Dealing with Conflicting Goals
- Guidelines for Attainable (SMART) Goals

TIME MANAGEMENT TOOLS AND STRATEGIES

- Schedules and Planners
- Common Electronic Calendar Features

MANAGE YOUR TIME IN ONLINE COURSES

- Manage E-Mail
- Manage Discussion Forums
- Manage Course Resources
- Manage Your Noneducational Computer Time
- Put Off Procrastination
- Develop Good Habits

ASK YOURSELF

Who are you and what are your unique skills and talents? What are your short-term and long-term goals and how do you plan to achieve them? What techniques do you use to schedule and manage your time?

IN THIS CHAPTER

you'll explore answers to the following questions:

- How can you set goals to strive for success?
- How can you create realistic goals?
- How can you use schedules and planners to help manage time?
- How can you effectively manage your time while online?

Analyze

Taking a self-assessment can help you think more deeply about your own skills and preferences. Consider the questions in this assessment and your responses. What information does this quiz provide about yourself that you can use to develop or improve important skills?

Rate Yourself as a Self-Manager

For each statement, circle the number that feels right to you, from 1 for "not true for me" to 5 for "very true for me."

▶ Periodically, I take time to think through academic and personal goals.	1 2 3 4 5
▶ I read each syllabus carefully to understand the course goals.	1 2 3 4 5
▶ I have a system for reminding myself of what my goals are.	1 2 3 4 5
▶ I find ways to motivate myself when I am working toward a goal.	1 2 3 4 5
▶ When I set a long-term goal, I break it down into a series of short-term goals.	1 2 3 4 5
▶ I have a system to keep track of my time on a daily, weekly, and monthly basis.	1 2 3 4 5
▶ I know myself as a time manager and what strategies work best for me.	1 2 3 4 5
▶ I record my tasks, events, and responsibilities and refer regularly to them.	1 2 3 4 5
▶ When I procrastinate, I know how to get back on track.	1 2 3 4 5
▶ I set priorities, making sure I focus first on what is most important every day.	1 2 3 4 5

Now total your scores. _____

If your total ranges from 38–50, you consider your goal-setting and time management skills to be strong. Reminding yourself of your important goals can help keep you motivated. You likely understand how to break larger goals into manageable tasks and how to keep track of your time, which is very important in online courses.

If your total ranges from 24–37, you consider your goal-setting and time management skills to be average. You may need to focus on your larger goals and how to break those into smaller tasks. By finding a time management tool that works for you, you can incorporate the strategies presented in this chapter to make the most of your time.

If your total ranges from 10–23, you think your goal-setting and time management skills need development. It helps to begin at the beginning—find out what matters the most to you and work around that. Set your large goals, break them into something manageable, and experiment with different time management tools to keep track of your schedule and your to-do lists.

Analyze: How can you make sure you set and attain worthwhile goals?

" Your academic and future career success
will require understanding yourself, your goals,
and your ability to manage your time. "

Despite having different priorities and responsibilities, many students commonly ask the same important question: "How will I get it all done?"

One of the major reasons many students give for wanting to take online courses is to save time, yet **managing time is the number one issue for most online students.** Though online courses make getting an education much more convenient by giving you a chance to learn on your own schedule, you can fall behind if you underestimate the time you need to devote. Often, if you fall behind in an online course, it is very difficult to get back on track, so it's best not to let that happen.

You only have 24 hours in a day, and at least 8 of those hours involve sleeping (or should, if you want to remain healthy and alert enough to make the most of the day). Though the idea of managing time may seem impossible, consider what it really is. In reality, you don't manage *time* at all. Time continues on no matter what you do. What you do manage are *actions within time.*

Time can seem to have a slower or faster pace, though. Have you ever done something that you love and noticed that time seemed to stand still—or even expand? When you engage fully in the important activities of your life, you may notice feeling more relaxed and productive, able to accomplish more than you ever thought possible. Sometimes the reverse is also true—it can be painfully difficult to accomplish a task, requiring much more time than it should. This phenomenon can be partially attributed to how meaningful each task is to you, personally.

The words of the 19th century German philosopher Friedrich Nietzsche, "He who has a why to live can bear with almost any how," illustrate why it is important to figure out what you value and how what you do in the moment relates to your larger set of goals. This chapter begins with a discussion about how to set important goals and then moves into how to use schedules and planners. The conclusion of the chapter focuses on how to establish good time management habits in your online courses.

A typical college student can easily spend about 10 minutes per page on reading from textbooks, articles, and websites. If you factor in doing assignments, watching videos, and listening to podcasts, you could spend 15 to 20 hours *per week* on one course.

Setting
Goals for Success

There's an old saying, "How do you know when you've arrived if you don't know where you're going?" Goal setting is all about figuring out your destination throughout the days, weeks, months, and years of your life. In fact, you probably set goals all the time and don't even know it. For example, you may not say, "My goal is to get up by 7:00 A.M. tomorrow morning," but if you set your alarm clock to wake you up at that time, you've set a goal.

What Is a Goal?

A goal is a statement of what you want to do, be, or have. Goals are intentions that provide clarity and focus for your thoughts, words, and actions. They can guide you to the specific outcomes that you are passionate about, given your values, as in the following examples:

Concentrated effort is a powerful force. Consider how light from a normal 60-watt bulb sends energy in every direction, but concentrated 60-watt light in a laser beam can penetrate metal. Goal setting can help concentrate your energy to reach a specific aim.

- *Fitness.* Improve eating habits; run two miles every other day.
- *School.* Sign up for the online program; get an A in my network security course.
- *Finances.* Save up enough money to buy new skis next winter.

What Is a Long-Term Goal?

Long-term goals sit out on the horizon, at least six months to a year away. They're goals that you can imagine and maybe even visualize, but they're too far out for you to touch. These are goals that reflect who you are and what is important to you. The more you know about yourself and your values, the better able you are to set and work toward meaningful long-term goals. Most long-term goals are far more achievable if you break them into smaller chunks. These chunks become short-term goals.

What Is a Short-Term Goal?

A short-term goal is a step that moves you closer to a long-term goal. Short-term goals make your long-term goals seem clearer and easier to reach. Short-term goals can last from a few hours or days to weeks or months.

Dealing with Conflicting Goals

To help determine important goals, consider your values, which are the central beliefs and attitudes that guide the choices you make. Though you may have multiple priorities in your life, including your family, friends, and health, there are some values that extend across most areas, such as the following:

Responsibility
Honesty
Commitment
Openness
Generosity

How are these values demonstrated in your educational endeavors?

Most people have several goals in different life areas. Prioritizing goals can be confusing if you think in terms of which is the most important. Over the long term, many of your goals are probably important, or they wouldn't be goals. When prioritizing, think in terms of timing: "Which needs my focus right now?"

When deciding which goals to start with, consider the following:

- Will achieving certain goals first make others easier to achieve?
- Do any of your goals express values that are more important to you than others?
- Which goals will create the greatest impact toward achieving your solution with the fewest resources?
- Which goals will create long-term results?
- Which goals have the greatest chance of success?

See Key 2.1 for additional suggestions.

Guidelines for Attainable (SMART) Goals

Anyone can set goals but that doesn't mean you'll achieve them. If you set "SMART" goals, you're more likely to succeed. **SMART** is an acronym for a list of qualities that make your goal more concrete and improve your chances of achieving it:

Specific

Make sure your goal includes as many details as possible to make it concrete. Focus on behaviors and events that are under your control and map out specific steps that will get you there. If you can answer the *What, Why,* and *How* of your goal, it is likely specific enough.

WHAT are you going to do? What action will you take (i.e., direct, organize, coordinate, lead, develop, plan, build, etc.)?

WHY is it important?

HOW are you going to approach it?

Additional Suggestions for Dealing with More Than One Goal at a Time

Stay focused. Don't set too many goals at the same time, and make sure that your goals are in alignment with your most important values.

Have at least one simple goal and one difficult goal at any given time. The simple goals motivate you as you accomplish them rapidly. The difficult goals keep you challenged and growing.

Have at least one short-term and one long-term goal at any given time. As with simple goals, short-term goals help ensure that you'll have frequent victories. Long-term goals keep you headed in the right direction.

Be flexible. Decide which of your goals (and tasks) are most important, but be willing to change a goal or even put it on hold for a while, if necessary.

Look for ways to combine goals and tasks. If you can work on two or more goals at once, you can consolidate your resources.

Stating goals in a positive, proactive way is more motivating than focusing on what you should not do. If your goal is to stop procrastinating, how can you say what you really want in a positive way? Saying "I want to move with speed and direction in all my tasks and responsibilities" is proactive. Negatively framed goals require not doing something and thus focus your attention on what you don't want instead of on a positive vision.

Measurable

Define your goal in a way that lets you measure it and create a way to evaluate your progress. This could mean keeping a journal, using an alarm system on your phone or computer, or reporting to a friend. Don't leave progress up to chance.

Though some goals are ongoing and may not in themselves be measurable, the individual tasks that you will later assign to these goals should be measurable.

Achievable

An achievable goal is one that you have the skills, talent, and discipline to achieve. If you stand reasonably good odds of accomplishing a goal, given enough time and effort on your part, it is achievable. This is not to say that goals should not be challenging, but you want the right level of challenge to avoid becoming overwhelmed or frustrated.

Realistic

Realistic goals fit in well with the other priorities in your life. Some goals may be attainable—you could accomplish them if you tried—but may not be realistic given everything else you want to do.

Timely

All goals need a time frame so you have something to work toward. If a goal is "a dream with a deadline," then without the deadline, your goal is nothing but a dream!

The following example demonstrates a SMART goal: I will sign up for a membership at the YMCA tomorrow morning. I am committed to attending three times per week for one hour each time. I will participate in a class, swim, or lift weights each time. I will schedule time on my calendar and keep track of how often I go and what I do. In six months, I will have gone at least 72 times.

Create a Path to Success

Here's an activity that involves an open mind and an imagination. Separately on paper or in a computer document, work backward to discover a path toward an important goal:

1 Name one important personal goal for this year. Using the SMART process, define and solidify your goal with attainable details that create a concrete plan for you to refer to. Remember to include the "SMART" breakdown:

Specific – Measurable – Achievable – Realistic – Timely

2 Imagine that you have already achieved your goal. How do you feel? How is your life different?

3 Imagine that a friend asks you to describe how you accomplished the goal. List at least three short-term goals that helped get you to the finish line.

4 Briefly describe some of the critical steps involved in achieving those goals.

5 Finally, tell your friend about the positive results that have come from achieving your goal.

Guess what? You just created a potential action plan. Consider putting the plan to work in the next year. When you do so, let the image of the success you created in this exercise motivate and inspire you.

Time Management Tools
and Strategies

Consider how well your current activities match your priorities and values. Examine the priorities shown in Key 2.2 and assess how important each category is to you on an A, B, C priority scale in which A is most important and C is least important. Fill in the chart with your rankings. Next, determine how many hours you spend on each of the activities during one week. Using a calendar, write in what you do each hour, indicating when you started and when you stopped. There are no wrong answers.

After a week, tally the hours you spent by category and insert those into Key 2.3. Compare the time you actually spend to your priority rankings. Do the hours spent on your activities match your priorities? That is, do you spend the most time on the most important categories? How would your activities during the day change if you took into consideration your priorities? Or are your priorities different from what you originally thought? Fill in the ideal amount of time per category on the chart.

Schedules and Planners

Goals and tasks don't get done on their own. You have to think about when you want to accomplish them. That's where schedules come in. Schedules aren't meant

KEY 2.2　Activities and Priorities

Activity	Ranking ("A, B, or C")	Activity	Ranking ("A, B, or C")
Classes	_____	Meals	_____
Studying	_____	Transportation	_____
Sleeping	_____	Relaxing	_____
Exercise	_____	Socializing	_____
Work	_____	Entertainment	_____
Family	_____	Computer activities	_____
Personal care	_____	Other	_____

to control your life; they're meant to provide some structure so you feel more in control of events by performing two important duties:

- Remind you of tasks, events, due dates, responsibilities, and deadlines.
- Map out segments of time for working on goal-related tasks.

Keep in mind that situations can change over time, and the reality is that most people's goals change over time in response to changed situations or new life events. Planners will help you manage and use your time to its fullest potential. Therefore,

KEY 2.3　Ideal Time Allocation

Activity	Ranking ("A, B, or C")	Number of Hours Spent in One-Week Period	Ideal Time in Hours
Classes	_____	_____	_____
Studying	_____	_____	_____
Sleeping	_____	_____	_____
Exercise	_____	_____	_____
Work	_____	_____	_____
Family	_____	_____	_____
Personal care	_____	_____	_____
Meals	_____	_____	_____
Transportation	_____	_____	_____
Relaxing	_____	_____	_____
Socializing	_____	_____	_____
Entertainment	_____	_____	_____
Computer activities	_____	_____	_____
Other	_____	_____	_____

Kirsten: Daytimer

Kirsten "couldn't get by without my Day Timer book." She puts everything in it—her contacts, syllabi, to-do items, schedules, and even recipes and other personal papers. Though it may not be the most high-tech option available and is getting heavier by the day, it works for her.

Marcus: Microsoft Outlook

Marcus keeps his personal and work schedules on his laptop computer through Microsoft Outlook's calendar program. He also keeps a running list of to-do items on the program and sets reminders for meetings and deadlines that appear on his computer screen at the time he determines. He always has his calendar open on his computer and refers to it often through the day.

Karen: Microsoft Entourage

Karen juggles a full-time workload as a marketing manager, kids' sports schedules, and her husband's travel schedule by using Microsoft Entourage for Mac. She can use a different color for each type of schedule: work, personal, sports, or husband's travel. Each Sunday evening, the family coordinates schedules, and Karen can see everyone's schedule at once.

you may have to adjust your schedule as you continually evaluate and reevaluate priorities.

You can use any number of systems to capture all the tasks, appointments, and projects you have to do. Your system may be a single sheet of paper, a calendar book, or a software calendar program. If you choose an electronic calendar, you may prefer a Web-based solution that can be accessed from any computer or you may prefer to use a program on your computer or cell phone. Remember that electronic options are known to occasionally fail due to software problems and battery deaths. Be sure to print or back up your schedules now and then. Many e-mail programs, such as Microsoft Outlook or Microsoft Entourage, also have calendar programs. The tool or system you choose should help you to be successful, relaxed, and in control of your time, but not limit you or cause you greater stress.

If you prefer to use a Web-based calendar that you can access any time, you can sign up for a free e-mail service, such as through Google's Gmail (www.gmail.com) or Yahoo (www.yahoo.com) and have access to the calendar programs. Click on the Calendar link on the home page to get there.

How do you currently keep track of what you do? Compare your answers with Key 2.4.

Common Electronic Calendar Features

If you select an electronic calendar program to manage your schedule, you can choose among the many available options. Most electronic calendar programs have similar features:

- *Calendar viewing options.* Most programs allow you to see your schedule by day, week, or month, depending on your preference.
- *Different calendar options.* You can set up different calendars—for school, work, personal activities, or your child's soccer games, for instance. You can view just one or multiple schedules at a time, with tasks color-coded by the schedule.
- *Add new events.* There are often multiple ways of adding new events. You can use menu options or simply click on the day in the calendar to open a new task.
- *Tasks.* A to-do list is a simple tool, but it saves you from wasting time worrying about whether you've forgotten something. Most electronic calendars allow you to list and prioritize tasks. For instance, high-priority items may be labeled as "A" or "1"—these are items that must be done. "B" or "2" items should be done after the high-priority tasks. "C" or "3" items are things you want to do but are not critical at the moment. Prioritizing tasks helps you to focus on the most important items first.

There is usually an inverse proportion between how much something is on your mind and how much is getting done. Everything from "complete term paper" to the smallest task such as "get gas" can pull at you. Writing down everything you need to do will help to move it from your mind and make it more likely that you'll get it done.

Regardless of the type of calendar tool you use, make sure that you incorporate course time into your schedule. Indicate as specifically as possible the hours that you will devote to your course—accessing it, reading, completing assignments, and studying. Make sure you allocate enough time per course (10 to 15 hours each week). Sharing your schedule with family members and friends will help them understand when they should avoid interrupting you.

No matter which system you use for keeping track of your to-do list, note the tasks for each day and prioritize them. Some people like to do this the night before so they can sleep better knowing they have a plan for the next morning. When you have a clear idea as to what you want to achieve for the day at its start, the chances are better that you will be able to proactively accomplish the tasks. As you finish the tasks, cross them off. Put any remaining on top of the list for the following day.

Manage Your Time
in Online Courses

Instant Message ▲

Look at me! I'm here to distract you from your course and all your other goals! ▼

Managing time on a daily basis can be hard enough, but doing so while taking online courses can be even more challenging. Some of the most time-challenging areas for most online students include e-mail, discussions, and course material.

Write down key due dates from your syllabus in one or more additional places that you will refer to regularly. Check these dates before you agree to any work, social, or personal commitments that could conflict with your school demands.

Manage E-Mail

In your online course, you will most likely have to e-mail other students and your instructor from time to time. You may receive important e-mails with tasks you need

Identify your goals for an online course. What grade do you want to receive? How does this grade fit into your long-term goals? With your goal in mind, and the idea that typical courses take at least 10 to 15 hours of your time per week to successfully complete, review the amount of time you will devote to the course. How and when will you fit the necessary studying into your schedule?

ONLINE
app

ONLINE OUTLOOK

TIM

Full-time accountant and father of two
Age 38

CHALLENGE

Not enough time in the day

I wanted to go back to school to get my B.S. in business administration in finance and decided the best way for me to do that was in an online program. I'm in my last term with just a few more assignments to go. The main thing that surprised me was the time my courses required. I used to think that online learning would take less time, but I have found that it actually sometimes takes me more time.

Almost everything seems to take longer online.

Even asking an instructor a question can take 2 days instead of 2 minutes; participating in discussions can be days, depending on the subject. You also can't rely on technology working whenever you want it to . . . something that should take 10 minutes might take 2 hours if the Internet is down or you run into some glitch.

It ultimately worked out best for me anyway because I saved a lot of time not driving back and forth and have been able to spend more time with my family than I would have been able to do otherwise.

to accomplish, and these e-mails may come directly into your inbox or through your learning management system (LMS). Key 2.5 highlights important tips for managing e-mail.

Manage Discussion Forums

Participating in required online discussions requires discipline. During a typical week, you might need to post an initial response to a question and then follow up by responding to what others have posted.

Check the course at the beginning of the week and read the discussion questions. Plan out an approach, such as the following:

- Writing your initial response and posting by Wednesday

KEY 2.5   **Tips for Managing E-Mail**

Check your e-mails every day. At a set time or times every day, check your e-mail in your inbox and in the LMS. You may have to check even more often if you are working on a group project.

Flag e-mails with reminders. Most e-mail programs allow you to flag a message and remind you to do something at a later time or date. Learn about this feature from the Help menu of your e-mail program and use it to your advantage.

Clean out your inbox daily. Most e-mail programs also allow you to create new folders. You can archive old messages in one generic archive folder or create specific folders to organize your messages.

Keep a copy of all messages sent and received. Keep all e-mail messages until the end of each course, at least. Organize your messages by folders in case you need to access them later.

- Responding to another's post by Friday
- Finishing any required responses by Sunday

Review Key 2.6 to learn practical ways to manage course discussions.

Manage Course Resources

Most online courses provide several resources, such as learning objectives, overviews, videos, audio podcasts, interactive learning objects, and lesson presentations. Familiarize yourself with all the standard features of the course. Then tailor the tools to your needs. For instance, if you like to listen to presentations on podcasts that you can download to your iPod or MP3 player, keep doing that, but if it becomes repetitive or you begin tuning out, you might want to use your time differently. If you are struggling with learning a complex concept and the course offers interactive activities or videos, use those to help decrease the time you spend trying to learn new material on your own.

Manage Your Noneducational Computer Time

Being online means having instant access to almost everything and everyone. You could have the best system in place to manage your time and be doing everything right, and then . . . you get an e-mail that someone has posted something to your social networking site, and you feel that you just have to respond. Before you know it, you're all caught up with everyone you know, but hours have gone by and you're not at *all* caught up with your assignments that are due tomorrow. Interacting on social networking sites can take a lot of time, so you will want to be careful about when you access these sites. Consider creating a new e-mail account specifically for

Bookmarks are Internet shortcuts for your favorite websites. Once you set them up, you can click on the bookmark instead of entering the Web address. Each Web browser has different steps to set these up. You may go to Favorites > Add Favorites (Internet Explorer) or click on the + sign (Safari). Search the Help feature of your browser to find its steps for bookmarking.

If you are stumped by a concept and the course materials are not helping, communicate that immediately to the instructor.

KEY 2.6 — Strategies to Manage Course Discussions

Check the online class web page every day to keep up with discussions. Consider bookmarking the class web page. Some web browsers allow you to create a list of websites that automatically load every day. If yours has this capability, put your course web page on this list.

Be sure not to use the discussion area as a social networking system. Manage your time in the discussions so you make sure to participate but also don't go overboard. You don't want to be online so much that it affects your ability to manage your time effectively.

Be considerate. Think carefully before you post a message. Correcting misunderstandings can take a lot of time and effort. When responding to a post, restate the message in your own words, say something positive first before giving any critique, and then give your thought-out opinion.

Seek to understand. As much as possible, let go of the need to convince someone you are right. Instead, try to fully understand why someone may have a differing opinion than you do. Understanding does not imply agreement; it offers mental challenge, and it can also save you time in the long run.

social network site notifications. While you are online, you can also set your status to "offline" or to "Do Not Disturb." Use these sites as a reward when you complete your assignments. Set a specific amount of time you will allow yourself to correspond with people, and determine when and under what circumstances you will use it. For example, you can tell yourself, "After I read and take notes on each of the three sections of this chapter, I'll check Facebook for five minutes."

Gaming, instant messaging, watching television shows or movies online, or talking on Internet video conferencing programs such as Skype can take a chunk of your time that you might not have planned on spending. Although a certain amount of downtime is needed, online distractions can become a problem when the time spent engaging in these activities grows too much. Close the programs when you need to concentrate on your schoolwork.

Put Off Procrastination

Even the most motivated person occasionally puts things off. It's only human to leave difficult or undesirable tasks until later. However, if taken to the extreme, **procrastination,** the act of putting off a task until another time, can develop into a habit that causes serious problems. For example, procrastinators who don't get things done in the workplace, besides preventing others from doing their work, may lose a promotion or even a job because of it. See Key 2.7 for strategies to help you avoid procrastination.

Develop Good Habits

Establish a Routine

As much as possible, try to establish a routine in which you work at the same times during the day or week. Start by identifying your most productive times of the day and plan to do most of your important work then. Most people know whether they're an afternoon or a morning person, but what a lot of people don't know is that it's a physical phenomenon, and there are real reasons for it.

Begin each school week on Monday, even if you only have time to glance at the materials and print out the schedule.

If you find yourself staring at the screen during certain times of the day, recognize that you may not be productive at these times and schedule something else. Likewise, recognize when you do get the most done.

Be Organized

Even a brilliant time management plan will run aground if you find yourself constantly looking for necessary items. Set aside a workspace and keep it organized so you can sit down at any time and focus on the work you need to do.

Computer folders and subfolders can help you manage your files. Some of the Microsoft Windows operating systems use Start > Documents whereas Mac uses Finder to keep folders organized.

Create an organization system on your computer. If you do not know how to do this, there are many resources appropriate for your operating system.

Windows and Mac each have websites that offer free tutorials. Do an Internet search for "managing documents in Windows" or "managing documents in Mac."

Back Up Your System Often (Famous Last Words)

You have probably heard this advice before, perhaps by someone who lost all their work because they did not take a few minutes to back it up. Save your data in another place (an external hard drive, CD, flash drive).

Analyze the effects. What may happen if you continue to put off a task? Chances are you will benefit more in the long term facing the task head-on.

Set reasonable goals. Unreasonable goals intimidate and immobilize you. If you concentrate on achieving one small step at a time, the task becomes less burdensome.

Set meaningful goals. When your actions are not in alignment with your important values, you can experience internal conflict and negative feelings such as stress, depression, fatigue, anger, or anxiety that make it difficult to accomplish anything. If you find yourself stuck for extended periods of time, look inward to see if you are being true to your values.

Try the 10-minute rule to get started whether you "feel like it" or not. For 10 minutes, and 10 minutes only, make yourself look at what you need to do, even if you just organize the project, read something related to it, brainstorm by yourself with just a pen and paper, or talk to someone about the subject. At the end of 10 minutes, take a break. Later that same day, use the results of your 10-minute session to set the foundation for 1 hour of concentrated focus.

Ask for help. Once you identify what's holding you up, find someone to help you face the task. Another person may come up with an innovative method to get you moving again.

Don't expect perfection. People learn by starting at the beginning, making mistakes, and learning from those mistakes. If you never make mistakes, you never learn and you never get any better.

Reward yourself. Boost your confidence when you accomplish a task. Remind yourself that you're making progress by giving yourself a reward—a break, a movie, whatever feels like a treat to you.

An easy way to do this is to keep all your working files in folders in one main directory folder (such as Documents). On a set day of the week, you can simply copy that directory folder. If you copy it to the same place every time, the computer will scan for changes to files and only save those files, taking only seconds to back up your work.

Prioritize

Use a planner to list each task you hope to accomplish. Set the priority of each task and check them off as you accomplish them. Your goal is not to do everything in one day but to keep aware of your obligations and priorities. In this way you will do everything in a timely fashion.

Vilfredo Pareto, a 19th century Italian economist and sociologist, developed a principle that has been used frequently. Pareto's 80/20 Principle implies that about 20 percent of what we do in any given area delivers 80 percent of the results. Going after the "right" 20 percent will get you 80 percent of the results.

Pace Yourself

When you spend a lot of time at the computer, it becomes more difficult, but more important, to take care of yourself. When working hard, take frequent breaks to eat and stay hydrated. This will help you process information faster and will save time in the long run. Get the appropriate amount of sleep that you need. You will be more productive if you do. Also make sure that you are eating well

If you find that you have problems saying no to requests, get over that hesitation now. No one benefits when you cannot fulfill an obligation you agreed to do or let your priorities suffer because of it. Say no confidently without being apologetic or listing all of your reasons. You have a right to manage your life.

Associate a new habit with an old one. If you drink coffee, make that first cup the time to write out and prioritize your tasks.

Embrace your inner elementary school student. For larger projects, post a chart of deadlines on your bulletin board or a calendar in your bathroom. Check each task off as you accomplish it and give yourself a reward.

Only handle things once. When you sort through papers, such as your mail, put the pieces into three piles: items that need action (put these on your to-do list), items to file for future reference, and recycling. Do this for your e-mail and voicemail, as well.

Practice the 5-minute principle. If there's anything you absolutely must do that you can do in 5 minutes or less, do it now.

Working toward goals and managing time are lifelong tasks. Your ability to successfully perform these tasks rises and falls according to your circumstances. Remember that you are not in this alone. When you seek help from the numerous resources available and especially from the people who are in place for support as you move ahead, you give yourself the best chance for success.

and getting the nutrition your body and mind need to function most effectively. Though you will likely not have the perfect life balance while in an intense educational program, strive to find some outlets that are important to you: physical exercise, spiritual practice, or anything that gives you a sense of vitality. Schedule periods of structured as well as unstructured time for rejuvenation, relaxation, and reflection.

Take Advantage of Downtime

You will literally spend years of your life waiting—in line, for appointments and meetings, for web pages to load, and so on. You can take advantage of these pockets of time. Keep a notebook handy to jot down quick thoughts that you might not have time to get into right away. Keep note cards and outlines around for review, continue with a reading assignment, or work on a problem set. Make incremental progress whenever possible.

If you have downtime in an airport, coffee shop, library, or other locale with wireless access, log in to your course and see what you can accomplish. See Key 2.8 for more tips.

If you watch television while you are eating dinner, consider watching a course video or listening to the course podcast during this time instead.

PRACTICE & plan apply

To get what you want, it helps to know what you want! The purpose of this assignment is to help you identify what your true goals are and to examine them, make them real, and break them apart into behaviors you can practice now.

What would you attempt to do or have in each area of your life if you knew that you could not fail? For just a few moments remove any obstacles that may exist and identify any important goals you may have been too afraid to admit that you have.

Reflect on each of the following categories:

- Work
- Community
- Play
- Spirituality
- Health
- Family
- Education
- Relationships
- Money
- Personal growth

Examine these categories and identify goals you have. Brainstorm (write anything that comes to your mind) for 10 minutes about how you would want your life to look if you could have anything you wanted.

PLAN

After you have finished brainstorming, spend the next 10 minutes looking over your list. Analyze what you wrote. If something is missing, add it.

Select your top three long-term goals (things you would want that will likely take one year or more to achieve). List those goals.

Reflect on how you chose your top three goals. Did you notice any common themes? What criteria did you use to pick these as your top goals?

APPLY

Now that you have a general idea for where you want to end up, generate an action plan for getting to where you want to be.

Choose one of your top long-term goals. List that goal.

Pause for reflection on your goal. What will it feel like when you have accomplished this? Describe your feelings. Is it a SMART goal? How so?

Brainstorm for 8 minutes about what you can do in the next year that will lead to the accomplishment of the goal. Write anything that comes to mind without judgment. There might be some strange ideas on your list, and that's OK!

Evaluate your list of ideas and choose at least three that you can accomplish in the next year that will lead to the attainment of your long-term goal.

NAVIGATING
Learning Strategies

3

USE ASSESSMENTS TO LEARN ABOUT YOURSELF

- Assess to Grow, Not to Label
- Types of Assessments

ASSESS YOURSELF WITH MULTIPLE PATHWAYS TO LEARNING

- Take the Assessment
- Apply the Strategies for Online Learning

ASSESS YOUR STYLE OF INTERACTION WITH THE PERSONALITY SPECTRUM

- Take the Assessment
- Apply the Strategies for Online Learning

ASK YOURSELF

When you take a course that you don't particularly like, what do you do to succeed anyhow?

IN THIS CHAPTER

you'll explore answers to the following questions:

- Why examine who you are as a learner?
- What tools can help you assess how you learn?
- How can you use your self-knowledge?

Analyze

Taking a self-assessment can help you think more deeply about your own skills and preferences. Consider the questions in this assessment and your responses. What information does this quiz give you about yourself that you can use to develop or improve important skills?

Rate Yourself as a Self-Knowing Learner

For each statement, circle the number that feels right to you, from 1 for "not true for me" to 5 for "very true for me."

▶ I believe I can develop my skills and abilities through self-knowledge and hard work.   1 2 3 4 5

▶ I have a pretty clear idea of my strengths and abilities.   1 2 3 4 5

▶ I understand which subjects and situations make it more difficult for me to succeed.   1 2 3 4 5

▶ In my course work and elsewhere, I try to maximize what I do well.   1 2 3 4 5

▶ I recognize that being comfortable with the subject matter isn't necessarily enough to succeed in a particular course.   1 2 3 4 5

▶ I recognize that it's better to have people with different strengths working together to accomplish goals.   1 2 3 4 5

▶ I assess the resources offered within a particular course and make adjustments so that I can learn effectively.   1 2 3 4 5

▶ I choose study techniques that tap into how I learn best.   1 2 3 4 5

▶ I try to use technology that works well with how I learn.   1 2 3 4 5

▶ I've taken a skills and/or interests inventory to help find a major or career area that suits me.   1 2 3 4 5

Now total your scores.   _____

If your total ranges from 38–50, you consider your understanding of how you learn to be strong. You feel confident in your study skills and can choose the best study techniques that work for you.

If your total ranges from 24–37, you consider your understanding of how you learn to be average. You will benefit greatly by understanding more about yourself and how you learn. Take the assessments in this chapter and follow the strategies to take advantage of your strengths.

If your total ranges from 10–23, you think you need to develop your understanding of how you learn. In this chapter, you will see the different ways people prefer to learn. After you take the assessments, you will have a much better idea about your own strengths and preferences and can apply the strategies.

Analyze: How do you best learn? Think of an example of your favorite or most effective learning experience and describe it. What was the method of learning? Was it lecture? A discussion? A hands-on activity?

> No one is good at everything, and no one likes every course, delivery method, or instructor.

Have you thought about how you like to learn? Even within the same class, different students have different preferences for how (and even when, where, and how often) they like to study.

Is it easier for you to learn new information if you can see it in front of you? Would you prefer to hear it? Do you find that you like to go to a particular place or environment to study?

Building self-knowledge about your preference for learning will help you become a better student and decision maker because the more you know about yourself, the more effectively you can choose the best courses and study techniques.

Knowing your learning preference can even help you adapt to situations in which your options are limited. Regardless of your preference, for instance, in an online class you may have to read materials on your own and listen to audio podcasts. You may have to participate in online discussions with others and write papers. With the self-knowledge you gain by taking the assessments in this chapter, you can develop strategies for dealing with information presented in ways that do not match your preferences for learning.

Use Assessments
to Learn About Yourself

Assessments have a different goal than tests do. A test seeks to identify a level of competence, whereas an assessment helps you obtain feedback about your potential skills, abilities, traits, or interests.

Assess to Grow, Not to Label

An assessment is simply a snapshot of where you are at a given moment. There are no "right" answers, no "best" scores, and your results are apt to change over time. The assessments you will take in this chapter provide questions that get you thinking actively about your preferences, and the strategies that follow each assessment can improve your ability to learn in online courses.

Understanding yourself as a learner will also help you appreciate how people differ. You can use what you know about learning differences to improve communication and teamwork.

Types of Assessments

Different tools can help you become more aware of how you think, process information, and relate to others. Some focus on learning preferences, some on areas of potential, and some on personality type. Three useful instruments assessing different aspects of these purposes are the VAK, Multiple Pathways to Learning, and the Personality Spectrum.

VAK

The VAK questionnaire assesses three learning modes: Visual (information in maps, charts, writing, and other representations of words), Auditory (information heard or spoken), and Kinesthetic (information gathered through experience and practice).

How can four students experience the same class in different ways? Consider the following four evaluations of one online course:

Student 1. I got so much out of the video lectures but I just struggled through the readings.

Student 2. I was confused until I read the essays. They were great!

Student 3. The discussions are always difficult for me. Seems like a waste of time.

Student 4. Talking about the concepts and responding to the comments of others in discussions was the best part of the course.

CREATE

Create a Character

Do you have a good idea already about your learning preference? Create a character and an activity to demonstrate how you typically approach learning something new.

The Multiple Pathways to Learning assessment in this chapter encompasses the VAK areas through three of the eight "intelligences"—visual-spatial, verbal-linguistic, and bodily-kinesthetic. Auditory learners who learn and remember best through listening should note that their strength is part of two dimensions (verbal-linguistic and musical).

In this chapter, we will cover the VAK learning modes within the Multiple Pathways to Learning assessment.

Multiple Pathways to Learning

Howard Gardner proposed a learning style theory in 1983 that changed the way people perceive "intelligence" and learning. His eight intelligence types encompass awareness involving bodily-kinesthetic, interpersonal, intrapersonal, verbal-linguistic, logical-mathematical, naturalistic, musical, and visual aspects. Multiple Pathways to Learning is a learning preference assessment based on his work.

Personality Spectrum

Different inventories and models have been used to describe learners' individual differences and their potential influence on the learning process. The Myers-Briggs personality types inventory identifies and measures four individual personality areas: extroversion/introversion, sensing/intuition, thinking/feeling, and judging/perceiving. The Personality Spectrum presented in this chapter is a personality type assessment based on the Myers-Briggs that can help you evaluate how you interact with people and situations.

Assess Yourself with
Multiple Pathways to Learning

You have your own personal "map" of abilities, which is a combination of what you are born with and what you have worked to develop. When you do what comes easily for you, you are probably drawing on one of your well-developed intelligences. On the other hand, when you have tried to do things that are difficult to master or

Intelligence		Description	High-Achieving Example
Verbal-Linguistic		Ability to communicate through language; listening, reading, writing, speaking	Author J.K. Rowling Orator and president Barack Obama
Logical-Mathematical		Ability to understand logical reasoning and problem solving; math, science, patterns, sequences	Physicist Stephen Hawking Mathematician Svetlana Jitomirskaya
Bodily-Kinesthetic		Ability to use the physical body skillfully and to take in knowledge through bodily sensation; coordination, working with hands	Gymnast Nastia Liukin Survivalist Bear Grylls
Visual-Spatial		Ability to understand spatial relationships and to perceive and create images; visual art, graphic design, charts and maps	Artist Walt Disney Painter Mary Cassatt
Interpersonal		Ability to relate to others, noticing their moods, motivations, and feelings; social activity, cooperative learning, teamwork	Media personality Oprah Winfrey Former secretary of state Colin Powell
Intrapersonal		Ability to understand one's own behavior and feelings; self-awareness, independence, time spent alone	Animal researcher Jane Goodall Philosopher Friedrich Nietzsche
Musical		Ability to comprehend and create meaningful sound; sensitivity to music and musical patterns	Singer and musician Alicia Keys Composer Andrew Lloyd Webber
Naturalistic		Ability to identify, distinguish, categorize, and classify species or items, often incorporating high interest in elements of the natural environment	Social activist Wanagri Maathai Bird cataloger John James Audubon

understand, you may be dealing with material that calls for one of your currently less developed intelligences.

As you read the descriptions of the intelligences in Key 3.1, remember that everyone has some level of ability in each area. Your goal is to identify what your

Each intelligence has a set of numbered statements. Consider each statement on its own. Then, on a scale from 1 (lowest) to 4 (highest), rate how closely it matches who you are right now and write that number on the line next to the statement. Finally, total each set of six questions.

1. rarely   2. sometimes   3. usually   4. always

1. ____ I enjoy physical activities.
2. ____ I am uncomfortable sitting still.
3. ____ I prefer to learn through doing.
4. ____ When sitting I move my legs or hands.
5. ____ I enjoy working with my hands.
6. ____ I like to pace when I'm thinking or studying.
____ TOTAL for **BODILY-KINESTHETIC**

1. ____ I use maps easily.
2. ____ I draw pictures/diagrams when explaining ideas.
3. ____ I can assemble items easily from diagrams.
4. ____ I enjoy drawing or photography.
5. ____ I do not like to read long paragraphs.
6. ____ I prefer a drawn map over written directions.
____ TOTAL for **VISUAL-SPATIAL**

1. ____ I listen to music.
2. ____ I move my fingers or feet when I hear music.
3. ____ I have good rhythm.
4. ____ I like to sing along with music.
5. ____ People have said I have musical talent.
6. ____ I like to express my ideas through music.
____ TOTAL for **MUSICAL**

1. ____ I like doing a project with other people.
2. ____ People come to me to help settle conflicts.
3. ____ I like to spend time with friends.
4. ____ I am good at understanding people.
5. ____ I am good at making people feel comfortable.
6. ____ I enjoy helping others.
____ TOTAL for **INTERPERSONAL**

1. ____ I enjoy telling stories.
2. ____ I like to write.
3. ____ I like to read.
4. ____ I express myself clearly.
5. ____ I am good at negotiating.
6. ____ I like to discuss topics that interest me.
____ TOTAL for **VERBAL-LINGUISTIC**

1. ____ I like math in school.
2. ____ I like science.
3. ____ I problem-solve well.
4. ____ I question how things work.
5. ____ I enjoy planning or designing something new.
6. ____ I am able to fix things.
____ TOTAL for **LOGICAL-MATHEMATICAL**

1. ____ I need quiet time to think.
2. ____ I think about issues before I want to talk.
3. ____ I am interested in self-improvement.
4. ____ I understand my thoughts and feelings.
5. ____ I know what I want out of life.
6. ____ I prefer to work on projects alone.
____ TOTAL for **INTRAPERSONAL**

1. ____ I like to think about how things, ideas, or people fit into categories.
2. ____ I enjoy studying plants, animals, or oceans.
3. ____ I tend to see how things relate to, or are distinct from, one another.
4. ____ I think about having a career in the natural sciences.
5. ____ As a child I often played with bugs and leaves.
6. ____ I like to investigate the natural world around me.
____ TOTAL for **NATURALISTIC**

Source: Developed by Joyce Bishop, PhD, Golden West College, Huntington Beach, CA. Based on Howard Gardner, *Frames of Mind: The Theory of Multiple Intelligences,* New York: Harper Collins, 1993.

For each intelligence, shade the box in the row that corresponds with the range where your score falls. For example, if you scored 17 in bodily-kinesthetic intelligence, you would shade the middle box in that row; if you scored a 13 in visual-spatial intelligence, you would shade the last box in that row. When you have shaded one box for each row, you will see a "map" of your range of development at a glance.

A score of 20–24 indicates a high level of development in that particular type of intelligence, 14–19 a moderate level, and below 14 an underdeveloped intelligence.

	20–24 (Highly Developed)	14–19 (Moderately Developed)	Below 14 (Underdeveloped)
Bodily-Kinesthetic			
Visual-Spatial			
Verbal-Linguistic			
Logical-Mathematical			
Musical			
Interpersonal			
Intrapersonal			
Naturalistic			

levels are, to work your strongest intelligences to your advantage, and to recognize which intelligences you can develop further.

Take the Assessment

The Multiple Pathways to Learning assessment helps you determine the levels to which your eight intelligences are developed.

Apply the Strategies for Online Learning

Nearly every person possesses some of each of the learning styles; however, most people gravitate toward one or two learning style preferences. Read through not only the strategies related to your preference but those that apply to all the intelligences. To achieve deep learning regardless of the situation, practice new behaviors and skills, be able to adjust your learning style when needed, and integrate new skills into your way of thinking and behaving.

Verbal-Linguistic

If you have linguistic intelligence, you are probably very good when it comes to understanding and manipulating language. You might like to read, tell stories, play word games, write things down, and discuss information actively with others. When studying, try the following:

- Take detailed notes when you read or work on the Internet.
- Describe what you think about different issues.
- Create flash cards to help you memorize material.
- Recite information aloud and develop stories around new material.

One of the benefits of online learning is that you can fairly easily adapt your learning environment to suit your preference for learning. Many online courses, especially those that have multimedia options, are geared to multiple learning styles.

The following list outlines other verbal-linguistic strategies you can use to study for an online course:

- *Use any multimedia presentations.* Go through any multimedia provided with your course or related to the topics, including animations, videos, interactive learning objects, and podcasts and focus on the words.

- *Print out transcripts.* If you are watching a video that you cannot seem to understand, try printing out the transcript so you can see the words.

- *Summarize.* After you watch something or go through an interactive exercise or animation, summarize what you have learned in note format within a word processing program. Keep your files and folders organized so you can access them easily. Outline text chapters and articles you read online.

- *Understand the course site.* Explore the navigation and organization of the course site. You can help yourself understand the layout of the course if you can view and print out the course map or create outlines of the course design.

- *Use multimedia technology.* Be creative in your assignments by using multimedia programs and digital recorders. While studying, consider creating crossword puzzles and other games to help you memorize. Many word processing programs have voice annotations, and your computer may have a voice recorder to help organize your thoughts. In addition, various desktop authoring programs and note programs offer helpful tools.

- *Selectively highlight texts and readings.* Whether you are reading online or from hard copies, highlight no more than 10 percent of the material.

- *Draw flowcharts.* Strengthen your comprehension of the logical patterns of course materials by drawing charts and diagrams that connect concepts together.

- *Move out of your comfort zone.* Do you find it more difficult to work with numbers and math? Try turning math problems into word problems. Tell the story behind the math.

Logical-Mathematical

If you are inclined toward logical-mathematical thinking, you work well with numbers and equations as well as logic problems. You are also probably capable of coming up with effective solutions for complex problems. When studying, try the following:

- Make charts or graphs of the information you have learned.
- Classify and categorize your notes and organize class materials according to importance to help you stay on task.

The following list outlines other logical-mathematical strategies you can use to study for your online course:

- *Develop systems and patterns.* Consider organizing your material logically and looking for underlying patterns in what you are learning.

- *Use gaming and problem-solving technology.* Make use of problem-solving and strategy game software to help you learn. Also consider exploring your knowledge of different programs, including computer-aided design (CAD), graphic calculators, and spreadsheet programs.

- *Use spreadsheets to organize material logically.* If it suits the topic, use a spreadsheet program to organize your notes.

- *Move out of your comfort zone.* Do you find it difficult to participate in discussions? Look for other like-minded people with whom you can discuss concepts. Find something about a discussion topic that interests you or find the patterns among related concepts within a discussion.

Visual-Spatial

If you have spatial intelligence, you are probably creative and enjoy art and drawing. Visual-spatial learners should make use of their love of pictures when learning material. When studying, try the following:

- Create pictures in order to represent certain terms or concepts from your class material.
- Sketch pictures alongside your notes to help you remember ideas, and create graphs and charts to visualize information.

The following list outlines other visual-spatial strategies you can use to study for an online course:

- *Take advantage of the visual media in your course.* Go through any visual media provided with your course, including animations, videos, and interactive learning objects.

- *Develop visual clues in the reading.* If you are reading online, take notes in a word processing program and use clip art, photos, or other visual aids.

- *Employ drawing and charting technology tools.* Use drawing, image composition, and paint programs. Apply charting, mapping, and diagram options in spreadsheet programs. Search for game software related to the subject area.

- *Use color.* Some programs allow you to assign different colors for categories or project filenames. Consider color-coding your notes.

- *Create a web portfolio.* Keep track of new material by creating a portfolio or website to demonstrate key concepts from each course.

- *Move out of your comfort zone.* Do you have trouble preparing for an exam? Try using your color-coded notes to study from or create charts with blank areas to test yourself.

Bodily-Kinesthetic

People with bodily-kinesthetic intelligence usually learn best by doing and love to work with their hands. When studying, try the following:

- Act out concepts from class.
- Link newly acquired knowledge with real-life examples.

The following list outlines other bodily-kinesthetic strategies you can use to study for an online course:

- *Digitally record notes and class material on an MP3 player.* Then listen to these recordings while walking, running, biking, and doing other forms of exercise.

- *Move while you learn.* Consider sitting on a ball or a rolling chair or standing up if you are learning at your computer most of the time. Take breaks from reading to pace and recite material.

- *Use any interactive features of the course.* Anything that allows you to move objects around the screen or to interact with the material while solving a problem online can help you learn it more easily.

- *Design and play active games.* Design a game that you can play to learn new material. For instance, you can develop your own hopscotch-type game, dancing game, or board game.

- *Incorporate movement in technology applications.* Software games that allow contact with the keyboard, mouse, joystick, or other devices can help you incorporate new material. Animation programs such as Flash can be good tools to help you integrate new knowledge.

- *Move out of your comfort zone.* Do you have trouble learning abstract concepts? Try creating a physical 3-D map of ideas by assigning different objects to different concepts. Move them around to better understand how they are interrelated.

Musical

Musical intelligence helps you understand the relationship between logic and creativity, particularly when it is manifested as sounds or beats. When studying, try the following:

- Listen to music while studying or learning.
- Create rhymes or mnemonics to help you remember important information.

The following list outlines other musical strategies you can use to study for an online course:

- *Write songs.* Turning material into a song or a rap can help you learn it. You can either create new music for your lyrics or use an existing score without words.

- *Create a rhythm from the words.* Beat out a rhythm with your hand or a stick while reciting concepts.

- *Use software to create music.* Use software programs that relate notes/sounds/actions with music. Create your own songs, using music and instruments, for any difficult concepts. Share the files with your classmates.

- *Move out of your comfort zone.* Do you find it difficult to excel at reading comprehension? Try summarizing concepts that you read in jingles or tunes at the end of each reading section.

Interpersonal

People with interpersonal intelligence relate well to others and enjoy discussions. When studying, try the following:

- Discuss course materials with classmates in online forums.
- Join an online study group.

The following list outlines other interpersonal strategies you can use to study for an online course:

- *Teach someone else.* Try teaching the material to another person. If you have a study group, you could take turns presenting information on new topics.

- *Connect with others by using technology.* As you study, discuss new information via chat or e-mail. You may want to make use of a video conferencing program, such as Skype, to help share information and connect you to others. You might consider having a study date online. Call a classmate and study together for a while. Sometimes just having someone else there, even remotely, can be motivating for interpersonal learners.

- *Move out of your comfort zone.* Do you have trouble studying alone? Pretend you are teaching someone else while completing the assignments or readings.

Intrapersonal

Intrapersonal learners prefer to study alone. When studying, try the following:

- Find a quiet place without distraction where you can learn effectively.
- Keep personal notes or a journal alongside your class materials to help clarify concepts and ideas.

The following list outlines other intrapersonal strategies you can use to study for an online course:

- *Reflect on the personal meaning of information.* Relate new information to something personal and seek a deeper meaning in the information for yourself.

- *Imagine assignments before you complete them.* Spend a little time before you begin a project or assignment to imagine how it will look in the end.

- *Use software programs to keep organized and solve any problems.* Brainstorming and problem-solving software programs can help you internalize new information. You may also find that video and audio editing programs fit your preferred style of learning.

- *Move out of your comfort zone.* Do you prefer to avoid group projects? If so, consider whether you undervalue the role that others can play in your education. Seek new ideas from other people. Set goals for interacting with groups, and make peace with the idea that it may be uncomfortable for awhile.

Naturalist

People with naturalist intelligence appreciate nature and can recognize many plants, animals, geological features, and more. You like being outdoors and find outside activities enjoyable. You can also categorize and classify things fairly easily. When studying, try the following:

- Find a place outside when possible to read and think.
- Find like-minded people in your course to interact with.
- Look for ways to classify information.

The following list outlines other naturalistic strategies you can use to study for an online course:

- *Look for relationships.* As in nature, there are connections among situations, events, ideas, and subjects. Look for ways that aspects of your learning fit together or do not fit together.

- *Merge observations and technology.* Use audio, digital, or video cameras to record trips for use in presentations. You can record, organize, and make calculations from data kept in a database or spreadsheet program. You can make use of multiple measuring and monitoring tools, such as probes, microscopes, and sensors that connect directly to a computer to help you collect data.

- *Move out of your comfort zone.* Do you find it uncomfortable to use spreadsheet programs or decipher graphs and charts? Try graphing or charting some patterns in nature and see how the visuals tell the story you know.

Assess Your Style of Interaction
with the Personality Spectrum

The multiple intelligences assessment focuses on your potential in areas of ability. In contrast, personality assessments help you understand how you respond to the world around you, including people, work, and school.

The Personality Spectrum assessment, developed using the MBTI and the Kiersey Sorter by Dr. Joyce Bishop, one of the authors of this text, scores on four personality types—Thinker, Organizer, Giver, and Adventurer. Look at the accompanying box to see skills that are characteristic of each personality type.

Take the Assessment

As with multiple intelligences, personality results may change over time in reaction to new experiences, effort, and practice.

Apply the Strategies for Online Learning

As with the multiple intelligences in the Pathways to Learning assessment and strategies, you can benefit from reading the strategies associated with each personality type and apply the ones that you think will work for you.

Thinkers

Thinkers learn from solving problems. They like to develop models and systems and often find new ways to approach materials or problems. See the following list for strategies that Thinkers can apply in an online course.

- *Give yourself time.* Thinkers like to have time to think things over and prepare for activities. Make sure you have enough time before a project or assignment is due. Stop periodically during reading to review and think of possible questions and applications. Leave some time before assignment deadlines, if possible, to review what you have done and the decision you have reached.

- *Have a reason.* It is especially helpful for Thinkers to know the ultimate goal. Understand all of the personal benefits you will achieve by undertaking a course or

Particular Abilities and Skills Associated with Each Personality Spectrum Dimension

Thinker
- Solving problems
- Developing models and systems
- Analytical and abstract thinking

Organizer
- Responsibility, reliability
- Neatness, organization, attention to detail
- Comprehensive follow-through on tasks

Giver
- Successful, close relationships
- Making a difference in the world
- Negotiation; promoting peace

Adventurer
- Courage and daring
- Hands-on problem solving
- Active and spontaneous style

STEP 1 Rank-order all four responses to each question from most like you (4) to least like you (1) so that for each question you use the numbers 1, 2, 3, and 4 one time each. Place the numbers in the boxes next to the responses.

4. most like me   3. more like me   2. less like me   1. least like me

1. I like instructors who
   a. ☐ tell me exactly what is expected of me.
   b. ☐ make learning active and exciting.
   c. ☐ maintain a safe and supportive classroom.
   d. ☐ challenge me to think at higher levels.

2. I learn best when the material is
   a. ☐ well organized.
   b. ☐ something I can do hands-on.
   c. ☐ about understanding and improving the human condition.
   d. ☐ intellectually challenging.

3. A high priority in my life is to
   a. ☐ keep my commitments.
   b. ☐ experience as much of life as possible.
   c. ☐ make a difference in the lives of others.
   d. ☐ understand how things work.

4. Other people think of me as
   a. ☐ dependable and loyal.
   b. ☐ dynamic and creative.
   c. ☐ caring and honest.
   d. ☐ intelligent and inventive.

5. When I experience stress I would most likely
   a. ☐ do something to help me feel more in control of my life.
   b. ☐ do something physical and daring.
   c. ☐ talk with a friend.
   d. ☐ go off by myself and think about my situation.

6. I would probably not be close friends with someone who is
   a. ☐ irresponsible.
   b. ☐ unwilling to try new things.
   c. ☐ selfish and unkind to others.
   d. ☐ an illogical thinker.

7. My vacations could be described as
   a. ☐ traditional.
   b. ☐ adventuresome.
   c. ☐ pleasing to others.
   d. ☐ a new learning experience.

8. One word that best describes me is
   a. ☐ sensible.
   b. ☐ spontaneous.
   c. ☐ giving.
   d. ☐ analytical.

STEP 2 Add up the total points for each letter.

TOTAL FOR   a. ____ Organizer   b. ____ Adventurer   c. ____ Giver   d. ____ Thinker

STEP 3 Plot these numbers on the brain diagram on page 46.

a program. Tie a given assignment to the learning objectives or the larger goal of career enhancement.

- *Participate in discussions.* You have more time in online discussions to examine issues. Question, probe, and look for the assumptions and conclusions others are drawing. Use the discussion and group areas in the online course to explore concepts with others. Propose problems and try to solve them with other people.

- *Convert material into logical charts, flow diagrams, and outlines.* Use a text editor or word processing program to organize new material and understand relationships.

- *Seek out facts.* Actively seek out external information to deepen your understanding of a subject.

- *Manage your time.* If possible, immerse yourself in individual subjects for longer periods instead of spending a short time on every subject.

Write your scores from page 45 in the four squares just outside the brain diagram—Thinker score at top left, Giver score at top right, Organizer score at bottom left, and Adventurer score at bottom right.

Each square has a line of numbers that go from the square to the center of the diagram. For each of your four scores, place a dot on the appropriate number in the line near that square. For example, if you scored 15 in the Giver spectrum, you would place a dot between the 14 and 16 in the upper right-hand line of numbers. If you scored a 26 in the Organizer spectrum, you would place a dot on the 26 in the lower left-hand line of numbers.

THINKER		GIVER
Technical		Interpersonal
Scientific		Emotional
Mathematical		Caring
Dispassionate		Sociable
Rational		Giving
Analytical		Spiritual
Logical		Musical
Problem Solving		Romantic
Theoretical		Feeling
Intellectual		Peacemaker
Objective		Trusting
Quantitative		Adaptable
Explicit		Passionate
Realistic		Harmonious
Literal		Idealistic
Precise		Talkative
Formal		Honest

Connect the four dots to make a four-sided shape. If you like, shade the four sections inside the shape using four different colors.

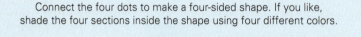

ORGANIZER		ADVENTURER
Tactical		Active
Planning		Visual
Detailed		Risking
Practical		Original
Confident		Artistic
Predictable		Spatial
Controlled		Skillful
Dependable		Impulsive
Systematic		Metaphoric
Sequential		Experimental
Structured		Divergent
Administrative		Fast-paced
Procedural		Simultaneous
Organized		Competitive
Conservative		Imaginative
Safekeeping		Open-minded
Disciplined		Adventuresome

For the Personality Spectrum,
26–36 indicates a strong tendency in that dimension,
14–25 a moderate tendency,
and below 14 a minimal tendency.

Source for brain diagram: Understanding Psychology, 3rd ed., by Charles G. Morris, © 1996. Reproduced by permission of Pearson Education, Inc./Prentice Hall, Inc.

• *Jump in.* One challenge for Thinkers is not to overthink something. Don't be afraid to jump in and start an assignment, even if you don't understand everything as much as you would like.

Organizers

Organizers like to have well-structured notes and clean study environments and learn best when assignments are clear. See the following list for strategies that Organizers can apply in an online course.

- *Understand the course organization.* If the course lacks structure or you need help in understanding how topics fit together, ask the instructor to help fill in any missing links or consult outside references. If your course does not include an overall layout, create one. Break your course down by week or unit. On one page or in a table, include all the readings and resources, types of assignments, and due dates.

- *Use a planner to schedule tasks and dates.* Your calendar should include all the assignments and due dates for the entire term.

- *Understand the assignment requirements.* Be sure that you understand the concrete deliverables expected for each assignment. If you do not, ask your instructor.

- *Categorize discussions.* Look at the discussion question and then look at all previous responses. Are there themes? Consider organizing each discussion topic by the general types of responses.

- *Organize course material.* Retype or summarize important points from your online or text readings. Keep notes from each resource or weblink you access.

- *Look for relationships.* Find connections among different ideas, events, situations, and subject areas. Identify the parts of the whole, if possible. Classify and compare what you are learning to understand what you already know.

- *Practice patience.* You might not always know how things fit together immediately. Often an understanding of how things are related to the big picture comes with time. Try to keep an open mind when things seem unorganized.

Givers

Givers tend to connect to other people and have successful, close relationships. They learn best when they are helping others in some way. See the following list for strategies that Givers can apply in an online course.

- *Participate in discussions and create study groups.* If there are not many opportunities for group activities in your online course, create them by seeking out students in the course through chat rooms or e-mail or setting up external chats and conferences.

- *Find others to teach.* Givers learn through teaching. Find opportunities to explain what you are learning to other interested people. If you have a group project or study group, take turns explaining different topics to each other.

- *Connect with instructors.* Though some instructors are easier to reach than others, interacting with your instructor will make you feel more connected with the course in general. Also reach out to advisors, tutors, and other support people.

- *Help yourself.* A primary challenge for Givers is that they tend to take on too many causes, always trying to help so many people that they don't have time for themselves. As the airlines say, "Put your own oxygen mask on first."

Adventurers

Adventurers tend to jump into learning, approaching it spontaneously and actively. They learn best from activities where they can try new experiences or become engrossed in competition or games. Adventurers typically like to be involved with other people, bouncing ideas off of them and solving problems as part of a team. See the following list for strategies that Adventurers can apply in an online course.

ONLINE OUTLOOK

SUSAN

**New online student
Age 42**

CHALLENGE

Social interaction

When I first signed up for my online program, I was a little afraid of the isolation factor. I thought I would be all alone at my computer and dreaded the idea of being lonely. What took me by complete surprise in my first online course was how close I felt to everyone else in the class. The instructor was right there the entire time, prodding me along. My father was ill for a short time, and I made a comment about this in the discussion area. My instructor sent me an e-mail the next week asking how he was and the rest of the students seemed so concerned.

I couldn't believe how much of a part of a group I felt with people I had never even met.

That was then, and this is now, though! I'm currently taking my second class, and it is an entirely different story. There is no group work, and nobody participates much in the discussion area. I have had to actively engage others and request study buddies. I didn't like doing that, but it seems to be working. I feel lucky to have had the first experience so now I know what it can be like. I will just have to put more effort into the social aspects of my courses if the course is not set up that way to begin with.

- *Seek out opportunities to participate.* Adventurers need a variety of new and challenging activities. Seek out information from other sources, experience the multimedia offered in the online course, and try out any of the games and activities provided. Use or develop your own games or puzzles to help memorize terms. Think of creative ways to learn new material.

- *Try things out.* Seek out opportunities to try things and experiment.

- *Participate in discussions and create study groups.* Adventurers typically like to be in the limelight. If there are not many opportunities for interaction in your online course, create them by seeking out students in the chat room, e-mailing others, and setting up online chats and conferences.

- *Take time to reflect.* Adventurers are pushed beyond their comfort zone when they are required to analyze and interpret data or have to read, write, or think on their own. Practice stretching yourself in these areas by regularly taking time to reflect on assignments and readings—ask yourself why they are included in the course, what you have learned from them, and how you can apply this new knowledge in other areas of your life.

Gaining self-knowledge can help you achieve greater success throughout your life. Besides helping you find ways to use your strengths on the job more readily, self-awareness can improve your ability to compensate for challenging areas when needed. Knowing how you relate to others increases your ability to work with team members. Choose to interact with people who have different strengths than you do so that as you continue through this text, through college, and into your life, you give yourself the chance to grow.

PRACTICE & plan apply

Based on the results of the assessments you took in this chapter, answer the following questions:

1. What kind of people do you get along with best?

2. What kind of people are more difficult for you to interact with?
3. How do you study best?
4. Given your personality type, what challenges do you foresee in taking online courses?
5. What adaptations can best help you succeed in your online courses?
6. How did the results of the assessments match your expectations? Were you surprised, for example, at being described as a thinker or adventurer?

PLAN

Look at Key 3.2 and begin to develop your personalized learning plan.

APPLY

Looking at your results for the Personality Spectrum and the Multiple Pathways to Learning, describe at least five ways you can enhance studying and learning in an online environment by taking advantage of each of your assessed styles.

KEY 3.2   **Personalized Learning Plan**

MY LEARNING STYLES PLAN

ASSESSMENT	What the Assessment Says About Where I Am	Learning Strategies Associated with the Style That Best Fits Me	How Online Education Fits My Style	How Online Education Differs from My Style
Multiple Intelligences Survey	My strongest intelligence seems to be:			
	I'm not so strong in the intelligence associated with:			
Personality Spectrum	My highest score is in:			
	My lowest score is in:			

CRITICAL Thinking

Programming

BECOMING A CRITICAL THINKER

- Take Apart Information
- Hear Other Perspectives
- Identify False Logic
- Neutralize Judgment
- Keep Out Bias
- Evaluate Sources
- Resolve Problems

CRITICAL THINKING IN ARGUMENTS

- Identifying the Conclusion
- Identifying the Premises
- Identifying the Supporting Evidence
- Identifying the Hidden Assumptions

CRITICAL THINKING IN AN ONLINE ENVIRONMENT

- Strategies for Using Critical Thinking in Threaded Discussions
- Strategies for Searching for Information Online

ASK YOURSELF

Do you think through your problems and decisions carefully? What actions help you tackle them successfully— and when you don't succeed, what gets in your way?

Analyze

Taking a self-assessment can help you think more deeply about your own skills and preferences. Consider the questions in this assessment and your responses. What information does this quiz provide about yourself that you can use to develop or improve important skills?

Rate Yourself as a Thinker

For each statement, circle the number that feels right to you, from 1 for "not true for me" to 5 for "very true for me."

▶ I discover information and solve problems by asking and answering questions.   1 2 3 4 5

▶ I don't take everything I read or hear as fact—I question how useful, truthful, and logical it is before I decide whether I can use it.   1 2 3 4 5

▶ I look for biased perspectives when I read or listen because I am aware of how they can lead me in the wrong direction.   1 2 3 4 5

▶ Even if it seems like there is only one way to solve a problem, I brainstorm to think of other options.   1 2 3 4 5

▶ I try not to let the idea that things have always been done a certain way stop me from trying different approaches.   1 2 3 4 5

▶ When I work in a group, I try to manage my emotions and to notice how I affect others.   1 2 3 4 5

▶ I think about different solutions before I choose one and take action.   1 2 3 4 5

▶ I spend time researching different possibilities before making a decision.   1 2 3 4 5

▶ I avoid making decisions on the spur of the moment.   1 2 3 4 5

▶ When I make a decision, I consider how my choice will affect others.   1 2 3 4 5

Now total your scores.   _____

If your total ranges from 38–50, you consider your thinking, problem-solving, and decision-making skills to be strong. Critical thinking is the most important skill a college student can have. The ability to analyze information to find out what is accurate and important and use it to solve problems will positively impact your future. Continue to hone your skills in these areas by concentrating on your weaker areas.

If your total ranges from 24–37, you consider your thinking, problem-solving, and decision-making skills to be average. It is quite important to develop the ability to think critically about information at this stage in your education. As you develop your skills for evaluating sources and identifying false logic, you will become a better thinker and problem solver.

If your total ranges from 10–23, you think you need to develop your thinking, problem-solving, and decision-making skills. Knowing where you are is half the battle to improving your skills. In this chapter, focus on the elements of critical thinking in terms of how to evaluate information and solve problems. Practice applying those elements at every opportunity, and it will soon be second nature.

Analyze: Studies have shown that the brain develops throughout life if you continue to ask questions and learn new information and skills. In what way do you want to improve your thinking in the future, and how will you do it?

> Problems and decisions, both big and small, come into your life every day.

In your life and college career, you ask questions and search for answers every day in order to solve problems or make decisions, as in the following examples.

- Responding to assignment questions by looking at the topics and thinking about available research sources
- Deciding between two banking plans by reading brochures and talking to the bank manager
- Offering an opposing opinion after listening to a friend's point of view

As you search for answers to questions, you transform pieces of information into knowledge you can act on. Where can you search for answers? How do you know whether the information you are relying on is accurate?

For centuries, information was archived and accessed through single locations—libraries—and an information seeker had to physically go to the locations, form queries in specific library jargon, and wait for the knowledge to be delivered.

Much has changed since then. The integration of the Internet with its full array of online information has transformed education, especially for online students who regularly have the Web at their fingertips. An information seeker today faces a constantly changing body of information, very different from the information that used to be warehoused in libraries.

In an evolving online world where anyone can be an author or post new "information," it is hard to find sources that you can trust. You need to be able to analyze an enormous amount of available information to determine what is good, what is misleading, what is completely wrong, and what is useful. This constant evaluation and use of information is the essence of **critical thinking.**

Becoming a Critical THINKER

There are multiple actions within the critical thinking process that you can use to examine an issue or work through a problem or decision. These actions form the acronym THINKER. See Key 4.1 for a summary.

| **T** Take apart issues and arguments | **H** Hear other perspectives | **I** Identify false logic | **N** Neutralize judgment | **K** Keep out bias | **E** Evaluate sources | **R** Resolve problems |

Take Apart Information

Break the information into parts and examine how the parts relate to each other and to what you already know.

T	**H**	**I**	**N**	**K**	**E**	**R**
Take apart information	**Hear other perspectives**	**Identify false logic**	**Neutralize judgment**	**Keep out bias**	**Evaluate sources**	**Resolve problems**
Critical thinking involves breaking apart information into parts. You can cut apart an issue or argument by identifying the conclusion, the premises, assumptions, and any supporting evidence.	To think critically requires that you are open to looking at things in new ways.	By learning to recognize faulty arguments and deceptive logic, you can improve your ability to think critically about issues.	Hold off from forming an opinion about something. If you form an opinion too quickly, you can close yourself off from the conversation and limit your ability to analyze an argument.	When you bring prejudices or preconceived notions to a situation, and those prevent you from thinking about the issue impartially, you have a bias.	Considering the source of information is crucial to determining if it is biased in any way.	The purpose of critical thinking is to take some action or make a decision. Applying the elements and a problem-solving format can help you resolve both large and small problems.

For any type of contentious issue or argument, begin by breaking it down into its elements. First, find the conclusion. Then, take a look at the form of the argument, identifying the premises and any hidden assumptions.

Hear Other Perspectives

One of the challenges in critical thinking is exploring how others think. It is possible that two people looking at the same thing can see it in different ways and both still be correct.

Do you see an old woman or a young woman in Key 4.2? They are both present. Your perception of each figure tends to remain stable until you can consciously change it.

Identify False Logic

By learning to recognize faulty arguments and deceptive logic, you can improve your ability to think critically about issues. The following are some common faulty persuasion techniques:

- *Ad hominem.* Trying to dismiss someone's argument by personally attacking the person who made it. If the reasons are good and the logic is good, then the argument is good regardless of who says it.

- *Generalizations.* Conclusions based on insufficient evidence. "I bought a pair of jeans from that store and they had a tear in them. That just goes to show you, never shop there—they sell defective clothing."

- *False dilemma.* Posing only two choices when there are a variety of possibilities and perspectives to consider. "Get an A in that course and you'll be set; anything less and you won't get a good job."

- *Appeals to emotion.* Summoning anger, pity, or fear to entice support. A scare tactic is one use of an appeal to emotion. "If you don't use that minty mouthwash, you'll have bad breath and no one will like you."

- *False appeal to authority.* Invoking quotes and phrases from popular or famous people who are not legitimate authorities in order to support a view. "I'm not a doctor, but I play one on TV. You should use this pharmaceutical drug."

- *False cause and effect.* Insisting that an event is caused by another event just because it took place afterward. "The stock market went up when the fashion industry shortened the length of women's skirts. They should do that again so the economy will improve."

Neutralize Judgment

For important medical decisions, the recommended advice is to seek a second opinion. If you can neutralize your judgment on other issues in a similar way, it will help you think more critically. Hold off on forming opinions based on just a little information and try the following:

1. Look at the process of forming an opinion as an internal argument with yourself, a mental debate. This means looking at all sides of the issue, pro and con.
2. Learn more about the subject by researching different sources.
3. Talk to other people, get their opinions on the subject, and weigh the reasons they feel like they do.
4. Read beyond the headlines on an issue. Often they are sensational and designed to get you to believe one side.

Keep Out Bias

Your emotions give you the ability to relate to others' experiences and serve the function of motivating you to accomplish difficult goals. They can be important ingredients to successful critical thinking. They can, however, negatively affect your ability to think critically if they are too strongly felt. If you have an extreme reaction to an issue or topic, take that as a clue that your ability to think objectively may be compromised.

Evaluate Sources

When you evaluate information, you judge whether an idea is important or unimportant, useful or not useful, strong or weak, and why. You set aside what is not useful and use the rest to work toward any personal goal—to create your paper, to solve a problem or make a decision, to support your ideas in discussion forums.

KEY 4.2   Optical Illusion

When critically evaluating websites and their information, consider the following aspects:

Accuracy

- Has the page been rated or evaluated in some manner? If so, who did the evaluation?
- Is the author's point of view clear and sound?
- Is there a bias—political, ideological, or cultural? Does the author hope to persuade you in some way?
- When was the site produced and last updated?

Authority

- Are the qualifications of the site's author or producer indicated on the page?
- Who sponsors the site? Is it a commercial or educational site, or does it appear to be created by an individual?

Completeness

- How well and thoroughly is the subject covered?
- Are the links appropriate, relevant, and comprehensive?

Content

- How many items are included on the page?
- Is a copyright notice indicated on the page?
- Does the site include a bibliography?
- Is the level of detail appropriate for the subject?

Propaganda

- Does the author present inaccurate or unfair descriptions?
- Does the author attack other perspectives?

Resolve Problems

Every day you may need to solve problems and make decisions, whether involving school (how to juggle your schedule to accommodate all your coursework), work (how to deal with a difficult colleague or boss), or your personal life (how to increase your income or deal with a medical problem).

A problem exists when a situation has negative effects, and problem solving aims to remove or counteract those effects. In contrast, decision making aims to fulfill a need. Both require you to identify and analyze a situation, generate possible solutions, choose one alternative, follow through, and evaluate its success. Key 4.3 shows the path that you can use to map out both problems and decisions, indicating your thought process at each step.

Creative Thinking

Creative thinking can help you develop potential solutions by thinking in fresh, new ways. Try the following to help improve your creative thinking ability:

- *Learn to brainstorm.* There can be dozens of ways to solve a problem or answer a question. Brainstorming, the art of considering numerous possibilities from the silly to the practical, allows people to explore a problem or an issue from many

Solve Problems Using a Plan of Action

Problem Solving	Thinking Skill
Define the problem: recognize that something needs to change, identify what's happening, look for true causes.	Step 1 **Define**
Analyze the problem: gather information, break it into pieces, verify facts, check the support, look for bias, evaluate information.	Step 2 **Analyze**
Generate possible solutions: use creative strategies to think of ways you could address the causes of this problem.	Step 3 **Create**
Evaluate solutions: look carefully at potential pros and cons of each, and choose what seems best.	Step 4 **Evaluate**
Put the solution to work: persevere, focus on results, and believe in yourself as you move forward.	Step 5 **Choose and act**
Evaluate how well the solution worked: look at the effects of what you did.	Step 6 **Reevaluate**
In the future, apply what you learned. Use this solution, or a better one, in similar situations.	Step 7 **Apply results**

different angles. Brainstorming will give you practice at keeping your mind open to new possibilities.

- *Think through ideas with others.* Once you have become comfortable with the process of brainstorming, learn to discuss your ideas with other people. Encourage them to open their minds and develop their own ideas and to help you critique and develop yours. This is an enjoyable part of teamwork and it yields the best ideas.

- *Look for the possibilities.* See situations in terms of what they can become, not what they are at first glance. In order to go in new and different directions, you have to visualize how things could be. Don't be afraid to come up with fresh ideas.

- *Make connections.* Creative people are good at seeing patterns in seemingly unrelated things. They perceive both similarities and differences and frequently come up with ingenious ways of capitalizing on a trend, a set of circumstances, or an existing need. Many inventions have been created from such flashes of insight.

However, watch for the pitfalls shown in Key 4.4 as you work to solve problems by using critical thinking.

Critical Thinking
in Arguments

Have you ever noticed that when you hear two sides of an argument, you find yourself being convinced first by one side and then by the other? Each position sounds good at the time, and you end up feeling completely confused.

The perfect solution. Believing that every problem has one perfect solution can intimidate you. If you can come up with fifty ideas, but none seems exactly right, you may want to give up. Don't look for the perfect solution. Instead, look for the best solution, using the time frame you have.

The smart people complex. If you run into a snag while trying to solve a problem, you might get yourself off the hook by deciding that only a much smarter person could solve this problem. Think positively. Believe that any person, thinking critically and carefully, can solve this problem.

The first choice is the best. If you come up with a good idea right away, it is tempting to go with it. Be sure to give each of your ideas equal time, even if the first one is good. Evaluate each so you can be sure you have covered every angle. The more solutions you generate, the better chance you have at finding the absolute best one.

Focusing on the "easier" cause. If you are not doing very well in a course, you may want to blame it on someone or something. "These online courses require too much discipline!" However, look for the true causes. In this case, it might be because you're not studying effectively or enough.

To avoid the condition that John F. Kennedy was talking about when he said, "We often enjoy the comfort of opinion without the discomfort of thought," it is helpful to have a framework to analyze arguments.

In your online course discussions and assignments, you may find many opportunities to engage in critical thinking. The following are common topics within discussions:

- *Moral issues.* Interpretations of the issues surrounding moral dilemmas, proposing a "should." ("We should get rid of the death penalty." "We ought to recycle.")
- *Predictions.* Analysis of previous evidence and observations to try to predict a future outcome or event.
- *Causal arguments.* Collection of evidence and observational data attempting to draw a causal chain between a series of events.
- *Problem-solving arguments.* Application of principles and past observations in order to propose the most effective course of action to solve a problem.

You can break each of these types of arguments into separate elements and look at them more closely. Some of the elements you will want to evaluate include the conclusion, premise or premises, supporting evidence, and hidden assumptions.

Identifying the Conclusion

A conclusion is basically the main point of the argument. It answers the question, "What are you trying to prove?" or "What is the main point?" Identifying the conclusion should be your first step in thinking critically about an argument.

"You should hire me because I have a great understanding of chemistry."

Conclusion: You should hire me.

Identifying the Premises

Premises are reasons given that will support a conclusion.

"We should increase taxes on the wealthy because we need to focus on infra-structure and building the economy."

What's the conclusion of this argument? We should increase taxes on the wealthy.

What's the reason, or premise? We need to focus on infrastructure and building the economy.

When you critique an argument using logical reasoning, you can only evaluate the strengths of the reasons. In the example above, you can look at the premise, "We need to focus on infrastructure and building the economy and argue why that is not true (the premise is wrong). Or you can argue why focusing on national needs does not require an increase in taxes (why the premise does not lead to the conclusion).

Identifying the Supporting Evidence

Supporting evidence may include proof of expertise or facts. A factual statement offers proof from a source that can be verified. In terms of logic, if a fact can be challenged, it then becomes an argument itself and not a supporting piece of evidence. Facts are facts only after they have been argued and generally accepted. If a statement is based on facts, it will likely pass one or more of the following three tests:

Fact: Over 70 percent of all Americans over 65 years have hearing difficulty. This fact passes two of the tests.

Can it be observed?

Has it been established over the years?

Can it be tested?

Identifying the Hidden Assumptions

An assumption links the premise and supporting evidence to the conclusion by answering the question, "Why does that evidence mean your claim is true?"

The assumption may not be spoken or written, but instead implicit, or hidden. Assumptions may be based on values that are thought to be shared with the listener or audience. The weakest part of any argument is its weakest assumption. If the assumption isn't valid, the entire argument collapses.

An example of an argument you may have seen on television:

You should buy our tooth-whitening product. Studies show that teeth are 50 percent whiter after using the product for 2 weeks.

What is the assumption?

People want whiter teeth.

Critical Thinking
in an Online Environment

A unique challenge of the online learning environment is the lack of face-to-face communication. Because students in online courses work independently, they have to be more "vocal." Many of the nonverbal communication mechanisms that instructors use in determining whether students are having problems (confusion, frustration, boredom, absence, etc.) are not possible in the online environment.

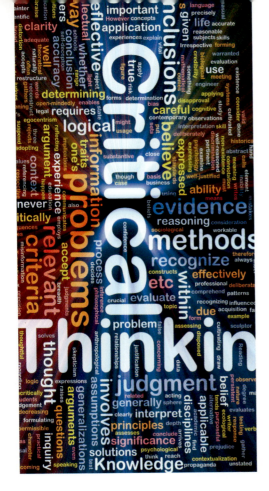

Strategies for Using Critical Thinking in Threaded Discussions

Many online courses offer threaded discussions based on questions, problems, debates, or situations and create an outlet for in-depth interactions that may require additional thought, investigation, or research. Threaded discussions do not occur in real time—you can read what others post and respond later. This gives you the opportunity to dig deeper into topics.

Many discussions will ask for your opinion on a certain topic. Apply the elements of critical thinking when making an argument and evaluating others' arguments in a discussion forum. Provide reasons behind your opinion. If people disagree with you, the burden will then be on them to debunk your argument.

While engaging in a discussion be sure to follow a few basic principles.

- Understand the goal of the discussion and its relevance to the course, your education, your life, and the lives of your classmates.
- Recognize the key concepts of the unit or lesson.
- Listen to others.
- Take turns and share work.
- Respect each other's ideas.
- Follow up on important issues after the discussion is over via e-mail or the bulletin board to take ideas to the next level.

Discussions can be hindered and stifled by an adversarial approach. Watch the tone of your language and err on the side of collaboration and nondefensiveness. Asking the right kinds of questions can help keep the discussion focused, lively, and nonconfrontational.

Key 4.5 shows types of questions you can ask in a discussion.

Strategies for Searching for Information Online

Evaluating information on the Internet is important because online resources vary widely in reliability.

When determining the accuracy and credibility of information on a website, it is helpful to understand the owner and his or her purpose in developing and maintaining the site. To find information about the owner, look at the title bar on top of the page. You can also look at the copyright information on the web page, usually found at the bottom.

About Web Addresses

You can tell a lot about a source by the web address. Most web addresses, also known as URLs, begin with http:// such as the following example:

http://www.mystudentsuccesslab.com

All URLs have extensions at the end, usually of three letters, that tell you something about them. The "dot com" in the previous example, for instance, is from the Pearson MyStudentSuccessLab website. The following list shows common extensions with their meanings.

.com   Usually a for-profit company

.org   Any type of organization, typically nonprofit groups

.net   Any type of company

.biz   Usually for small businesses

.gov   Governmental agency

.edu   Typically for higher education (university, community college, for-profit technical school, etc.)

.info   A reputable source of information

Some web extensions indicate the country where the site originates. For example, .us is for sites in the United States, .uk for United Kingdom, .de for Germany, and .cn is for China.

Other common extensions seen regularly include .mobi for sites optimized for mobile browsing devices and .tv for multimedia sites, often belonging to entertainment companies.

CARS

Robert Harris, professor and Web expert, has developed an easy-to-remember system for evaluating Internet information called the CARS test for information quality (Credibility, Accuracy, Reasonableness, Support). Use the information in Key 4.6 to question any source you find while conducting research. The same system can also help test the reliability of non-Internet sources.

KEY 4.5   **Questions to Ask in Discussion Forums**

Clarify the meaning of vocabulary or terms. After reading another's post, summarize in your own words what was said so the meaning is clear to all. If necessary, ask questions for clarification.

- What do you mean by _____?
- Could you give me an example?
- How does this relate to _____?

Break apart the question or issue. You may want to find out more about the topic and break it down into its conclusion, premises, assumptions, and supporting evidence. Examples:

- What does this question assume?
- Does this issue lead to other questions or issues?
- You seem to be assuming _____. Is that right?
- Do you have evidence for that?
- How could we find out if that is true?
- What is the source for the evidence?
- Why do you believe the information source is reliable?

Look for causes and effects. If a discussion participant draws a conclusion, you may want to take it further and examine what happens if the conclusion is indeed true. Ask questions such as the following:

- What effect would that have?
- What alternatives are there?
- If that is the case, then what follows?
- What are the causes of that?
- If another action is taken, is the effect still the same?

Examine perspectives and viewpoints. There will often be multiple viewpoints in a discussion forum. See whether you can understand other views. Questions like the following can help with that:

- What caused you to feel that way?
- How do you respond to people who disagree with your ideas?
- Can you explain what influenced you to think _____?
- How would you respond to the objection that _____?

Credibility	Accuracy	Reasonableness	Support
Examine whether a source is believable and trustworthy.	**Examine whether information is correct— i.e., factual, comprehensive, detailed, and up to date (if necessary).**	**Examine whether material is fair, objective, moderate, and consistent.**	**Examine whether a source is adequately supported with citations.**
What are the author's credentials?	**Is it up to date, and is that important?**	**Does the source seem fair?**	**Where does the information come from?**
Look for education and experience, title or position of employment, membership in any known and respected organization, reliable contact information, biographical information, and reputation.	If you are searching for a work of literature, such as Shakespeare's play *Macbeth,* there is no "updated" version. However, you may want reviews of its latest productions. For most scientific research, you will need to rely on the most updated information you can find.	Look for a balanced argument, accurate claims, and a reasoned tone that does not appeal primarily to your emotions.	Look at the site, the sources used by the person or group who compiled the information, and the contact information. Make sure that the cited sources seem reliable and that statistics are documented.
Is there quality control?	**Is it comprehensive?**	**Does the source seem objective?**	**Is the information corroborated?**
Look for ways in which the source may have been screened. For example, materials on an organization's website have most likely been approved by several members; information coming from an academic journal has to be screened by several people before it is published.	Does the material leave out any important facts or information? Does it neglect to consider alternative views or crucial consequences? Although no one source can contain all of the available information on a topic, it should still be as comprehensive as is possible within its scope.	While there is a range of objectivity in writing, you want to favor authors and organizations who can control their bias. An author with a strong political or religious agenda or an intent to sell a product may not be a source of the most truthful material.	Test information by looking for other sources that confirm the facts in this information— or, if the information is opinion, sources that share that opinion and back it up with their own citations. One good strategy is to find at least three sources that corroborate each other.
Is there any posted summary or evaluation of the source?	**For whom is the source written, and for what purpose?**	**Does the source seem moderate?**	**Is the source externally consistent?**
You may find abstracts of sources (summary) or a recommendation, rating, or review from a person or organization (evaluation). Either of these—or, ideally, both— can give you an idea of credibility before you decide to examine a source in depth.	Looking at what the author wants to accomplish will help you assess whether it has a bias. Sometimes biased information will not be useful for your purpose; sometimes your research will require that you note and evaluate bias (such as if you were to compare Civil War diaries from Union soldiers with those from Confederate soldiers).	Do claims seem possible, or does the information seem hard to believe? Does what you read make sense when compared to what you already know? While wild claims may turn out to be truthful, you are safest to check everything out.	Most material is a mix of both current and old information. External consistency refers to whether the old information agrees with what you already know. If a source contradicts something you know to be true, chances are higher that the information new to you may be inconsistent as well.
Signals of a potential lack of credibility:	**Signals of a potential lack of accuracy:**	**Signals of a potential lack of reasonableness:**	**Signals of a potential lack of support:**
Anonymous materials, negative evaluations, little or no evidence of quality control, bad grammar or misspelled words	Lack of date or old date, generalizations, one-sided views that do not acknowledge opposing arguments	Extreme or emotional language, sweeping statements, conflict of interest, inconsistencies or contradictions	Statistics without sources, lack of documentation, lack of corroboration using other reliable sources

Source: Robert Harris, "Evaluating Internet Research Sources," November 17, 1997, VirtualSalt (www.virtualsalt.com/evalu8it.htm).

Consider the following two discussion posts and identify which approach better uses critical thinking skills. Identify at least two specific ways that both posts could be more effective. Then compose a response to one of the posts using the questions from this section.

Question

What age are the baby boomers now? What positive and negative impacts do you think the "boomer" generation has—and will have—on subsequent generations (i.e., social, educational, economic, environmental, and political resources)? What can be done now to mitigate any negative future impacts? Post websites and use your text, life experience, media and news, and other information to back your position.

Sample Post 1

The Baby Boom started after the Second World War and ended somewhere around the beginning to middle 1960s. That would make the baby boomers roughly 47 to 64 years of age at this time. "Studies show that the impacts brought about by the society where baby boomers grew up contributes a lot in reshaping society" (Mitchell, 2008).

The "boomer" generation came about when soldiers returning from the war found that life was much easier at home. There were more jobs and houses were easily acquired. Because of the prosperous time, people were able to have large families and support them. Because of their sheer numbers, this generation has played a major positive role in the changes of social structures in the United States, namely in finance, family, work ethic, and popular culture, including how ads are targeted to specific groups. Although the Boomers have had many positive influences on the world, there are clearly some negative effects that need to be understood to prepare society for the future. The social effects the Baby Boomers have had on finance, family, work ethic, and today's popular culture have, in many ways, weakened the integrity and value systems of subsequent generations. The changes in social security, health care, and the retirement age may be difficult to undo, but we must put strategies in place to revert these to their original conceptions in order to mitigate the negative effects the changes will have in the future.

References

http://www.ageworks.com/course_demo/200/module2/module2b
http://www.geography.hunter.cuny.edu/age.structure.outline
http://ezinearticles.com/?Impact-of-Baby-Boomers-on-American-Society&id=932508

Sample Post 2

The baby boomers are in their 60s. All the money I pay for social security is going to get eaten up by the large population of boomers. My generation may never actually see our social security plan.

When researching online, keep the following strategies in mind:

- *Stay focused on the big picture.* In examining the specifics and tangents you find while doing online searches, stay clear about the overall purpose.

- *Examine assumptions and biases, including your own.* Understanding the author's intended audience may help you understand the assumptions and biases in what you read.

- *Use Wikipedia and other wikis carefully.* Wikis are web pages that can be modified by anyone with a web browser. One of the most popular, Wikipedia, is an online, editable collection of facts and opinions. Wikis can be useful for online collaboration, getting clarification of ideas, or finding suggestions for research, but they cannot replace authorized sources of information. Most wikis can be reviewed and

Evaluate Websites

Choose at least three websites hosted at different extensions (.com, .org, .net, etc.) that cover the same subject matter and evaluate the apparent reliability of the sites based on the criteria of the CARS test.

edited by anyone, anonymously. There is no way to determine the authorship or expertise behind the ideas. This means that they can be very accurate or grossly inaccurate, and most instructors will not accept them as references.

- *Be aware of false arguments.* In your search for information, be on the lookout for faulty logic and persuasion techniques.

- *Use the checklist of criteria.* The checklist in this chapter will help you evaluate Internet sources. Use the criteria that are most helpful, and get in the habit of looking for all of the elements. Even if the technology changes, your criteria for good information will not.

- *Make sure to paraphrase.* You can't just directly copy material gathered from the websites you use for papers, discussions, and other assignments. Moreover, you still need to reference the sites that helped you find the data, understand concepts, get research ideas, and so on. A helpful method is to list all relevant web addresses at the bottom of your post or in footnotes or endnotes of a formal essay.

- *Distinguish peer-reviewed sources from non-peer-reviewed sources.* When an article, website, or other information source goes through a review and editing process by others in the field, it is referred to as peer reviewed. This process gives added assurance that the material is reliable.

- *Ask your instructor.* If you are ever unsure of the scholarly value of a website, ask the teacher of your course.

ONLINE OUTLOOK

ALEXA

Age 21

CHALLENGE

Selling myself short

I turned in a three-page paper in one of my first courses in which I argued my opinion on why HIPAA is too stringent. I just got it back with this comment in the subject line:

"Don't sell yourself short!"

I had to search for why the instructor wrote this, but at the end of the paper I saw the explanation. In my three-page assignment, I had argued all of the reasons to justify what I thought of HIPAA, and my closing statement was, "but, that's just my opinion." My instructor wrote in the comment box that I was completely wrong! I thought he was arguing about HIPAA, but he was actually telling me that since I had argued my points so well, it was no longer just an opinion, it was a solid argument.

I had never thought about that before, but I had created a genuine, structured argument backed up with solid reasons.

I was impressed with myself, actually!

You can use critical thinking and problem solving to evaluate many situations in your life. Practice these skills by choosing one of the following scenarios to examine:

a. Jamie, a full-time online student who also works 25 hours a week, is beginning to fall behind in her studies. What can she do?

b. Jordan is having trouble understanding the content in one of his technical courses. He's reading the course material online, reading the textbook, doing the assignments and homework, but it is still confusing. What can he do?

c. Renee is experiencing a problem with her boss at work. The evaluations she has been receiving do not seem fair. What should she do?

d. Maria is carrying a full course load, working part time, and trying to raise three children on her own. She can't seem to get to her coursework in time to finish it every week. How should she approach this problem?

e. John is not doing well in his online course. This is the first online course he has taken, and although the material is not very difficult, he cannot seem to motivate himself to get through it. He recognizes education is the key to his future, and this type of program can fit into his already hectic life. What can he do about this situation?

f. Other. Choose a problem you are currently facing that you would like to solve.

PLAN

Using the problem-solving method presented in this chapter, evaluate the scenario you have chosen.

Define
What are the facts of the situation? Name the problem specifically without focusing on causes or effects.

Analyze
Analyze the problem. Gather information, break it into pieces, verify facts, check the support, look for bias, evaluate information.

Create
Generate possible solutions, using creative strategies to think of ways you could address the causes of this problem.

Evaluate
Evaluate solutions. Look carefully at potential pros and cons of each, and choose what seems best.

APPLY

Select the best solution. Detail how you can evaluate whether the solution worked.

ONLINE READING,
Information Literacy, and Study Skills

Uploading Information

GET READY TO READ

- Define Your Purpose
- Be Prepared for a Challenge
- Set Realistic Goals
- Expand Your Vocabulary
- Deal with Internal Distractions
- Prepare for Online Reading

ACTIVE READING STRATEGIES

- Rapidly Skim
- Evoke Memories
- Apply Critical Thinking
- Determine Main Ideas
- Engage with Others
- Review
- Summarize

ONLINE READING CHALLENGES

- Complex Material
- Eyestrain
- Reading Strategies for Different Learning Styles

ASK YOURSELF

What strategies help you absorb material? How do those strategies change depending on whether you read printed or online material?

IN THIS CHAPTER

you'll explore answers to the following questions:

- What sets you up for reading comprehension?
- How can you skim material to quickly assess the content?
- How can you respond critically to what you read?
- How can you use your learning style to your advantage when reading online material?

Analyze

Taking a self-assessment can help you think more deeply about your own skills and preferences. Consider the questions in this assessment and your responses. What information does this quiz provide about yourself that you can use to develop or improve important skills?

Rate Yourself as a Reader of Online and Text Materials

For each statement, circle the number that feels right to you, from 1 for "not true for me" to 5 for "very true for me."

▶ If my school required a Web navigation test for entry, I could easily pass. I know how to make my way around the Web.   1 2 3 4 5

▶ I like to skim through any material I'm about to read first.   1 2 3 4 5

▶ I keep my reading objective in mind as I click through the Web.   1 2 3 4 5

▶ I pay attention to multimedia on the websites I'm reading.   1 2 3 4 5

▶ I believe that, if I take my time, I can understand almost anything that I have to read for school.   1 2 3 4 5

▶ I always like to find out how new information I'm reading is directly related to me.   1 2 3 4 5

▶ I'm very aware of the source of information—I look at the websites where I find material and wonder who put it there and why.   1 2 3 4 5

▶ Building a larger vocabulary is important to me.   1 2 3 4 5

▶ I am good at finding the main ideas of the paragraphs I read.   1 2 3 4 5

▶ I know how to take notes in another file while I'm reading online.   1 2 3 4 5

Now total your scores.   _____

If your total ranges from 38–50, you consider your reading skills for text and online material to be strong. Reading for online courses will often require reading onscreen and reading from text materials. It's important as you approach any reading assignment to keep your purpose in mind, skim the material first, find the main ideas, and continue to build your vocabulary.

If your total ranges from 24–37, you consider reading skills for text and online material to be average. Make sure that you build on your current skills to read and navigate onscreen content and material in print. This chapter will present a different strategy to use for each. Continue to hone your reading comprehension skills by practicing each.

If your total ranges from 10–23, you think you need to develop your reading skills for text and online material. Perhaps you feel like you are challenged mainly in the online reading area or you may feel that your skills for both print and online material need improvement. Concentrate on practicing the strategies presented in this chapter to begin to develop the skills you will use for the rest of your life.

Analyze: How important do you think reading skills are? Why? In what way would you like to improve your reading skills?

> *Taking online classes requires mastering a variety of reading and studying skills, depending on the content, the instructor, and the media used.*

Colleges have high expectations regarding your reading and studying habits. College reading assignments, whether textbook chapters, journal articles, or other materials, are often long and challenging. Though the instructor will not be hanging over your shoulder to make sure you do your reading, you will be held responsible for demonstrating what you've learned in the form of discussions, presentations, projects, papers, and exams.

Many online courses require you to effectively read printed material as well as online material. In addition to your textbook, which may be printed or electronic, your course may also require you to read digital articles and online news and current events. You may also need to read a variety of material gathered during research from an online library or Web search.

College-level reading is demanding enough in itself, but reading online presents additional challenges. You have to navigate words, pictures, videos, animations, sounds, hypertext, interactive learning media, and more without becoming so distracted that you lose your purpose for reading. Within a single article published on a website, there may be a news report, a narrated photo slideshow with captions, streaming video, a blog report, and links to related articles.

When reading online you have to make continual judgment calls about which information to look at. There may not be a clear beginning, middle, and end. How do you know what to focus on? Are the media and text being used to communicate a particular view? Is that view accurate? In an online environment, not only do you have to be a good reader to extract useful information, but you also have to be a good critical thinker.

For all its challenges, the ability to read well online also has advantages. Reading a few valid websites, an op-ed article, and a blog post can sometimes lead you to what you need more quickly and in a more focused way than if you were reading an entire book page by page.

The ability to read digital text well can also benefit your career. It is a highly desirable ability in the digital-age job market. Department of Education statistics show that those who score higher on online reading tests tend to earn higher incomes. With over 60 million U.S. workers now spending more than 2 hours a day reading directly from a computer display, learning how to be a good reader at this point in your education can have long-term benefits for your career.*

A 2006 survey by the Conference Board, which conducts research for business leaders, found that nearly 90 percent of employers rated reading comprehension as "very important."[†]

Get Ready
to Read

Before you even open a book, electronic document, or web page, how can you get ready to make the most of your reading? Build a useful mindset with the following steps and strategies.

*Rich, M. (2008, July 27). Literacy Debate: Online, R U Really Reading? *The New York Times*. Retrieved from www.nytimes.com/2008/07/27/books/27reading.html?pagewanted=1&_r=3

[†]The Conference Board. (2006). Are They Ready to Work? Employers' Perspectives on the Basic Knowledge and Applied Skills of New Entrants to the 21st Century U.S. Workforce. Retrieved from www.conference-board.org/pdf_free/BED-06-workforce.pdf

Define Your Purpose

If you have questions, contact your instructor immediately. Don't wait or rely on other students if you do not understand the purpose of a reading or what is expected of you. Get answers from your instructor right away.

Know why you are reading what you are reading: To comprehend concepts and details? To evaluate critically? To learn how to do something? Find out how the reading will be used. Is it for a discussion or assignment? If so, review the discussion topics or guidelines first.

Be Prepared for a Challenge

The material might not click right away. Be patient. When you first begin, there is usually some uncertainty that you will have to tolerate. Keep reading and see whether you understand more.

Set Realistic Goals

Select a reasonable chunk of material to read in one sitting. You don't want to overtax yourself or expect that you'll be able to comprehend an enormous amount of material in a short amount of time. Pace yourself. A successful strategy employed by many students is to read for no longer than 20 minutes in one sitting. Then take a break and test your comprehension before sitting down for another reading session. Many students find that they can comprehend about five to ten pages of college-level material per hour. Set realistic goals and give yourself enough time.

Expand Your Vocabulary

Every subject has its own specialized vocabulary. Even if you feel like you are diving into a foreign language, know that the more you see these terms, the more you will remember and understand them. Use an online dictionary (such as the one at www.dictionary.com). Most word processing programs also have dictionaries and thesauruses. To help solidify your understanding of new terms, try making flash cards, a glossary, or simply using the words in your own sentences.

Deal with Internal Distractions

Internal distractions will disrupt your concentration. When worries come up, like scheduling concerns or reminders for your to-do list, write them down to deal with later. Or take a break if a problem seems more urgent. Exercise may help, music may relieve stress, or a snack can reduce hunger.

Prepare for Online Reading

Take Control of Technology

Don't Web surf, e-mail, instant message, or download songs onto your iPod while you are trying to read. If you are using an online reading program or library, explore the features of the system. Learn how to view the table of contents, flip pages, move around the document, highlight and take notes, and adjust the view. The more you know your platform, the less technology issues will interfere with your learning as you read. Also, know whether you need an Internet connection. Some textbooks "live" online, whereas others are downloaded to your computer or device. Make sure you will have Internet access when you need it or print out a copy to read if you won't.

Printed Material

Most textbooks also include elements that provide a big picture overview of the main ideas and themes. These can include any or all of the following:

- *Front matter.* The table of contents shows the chapter titles, the main topics in each chapter, and the order in which they will be covered, as well as special features. In the preface the author tells you what the book will cover and its point of view.
- *Chapter introductions or outlines.* Lists of objectives or key topics are found at the beginnings of chapters.
- *Different styles or arrangements of type.* Boldface, italics, underlining, larger fonts, bullet points, or boxed text can flag vocabulary or important ideas.
- *End-of-chapter summaries.* A review of chapter content and main ideas is often used to conclude the chapter text.
- *Margin materials.* Definitions, quotes, questions, and exercises are useful additions to text material.
- *Sidebars or boxed features.* Special inserts set off from text are usually connected to text themes and introduce extra tidbits of information that supplement the text.
- *Review questions and exercises.* Items that test your knowledge help you understand and apply content in creative and practical ways.

E-Books and Online Material

In addition to the same elements you can find in printed text, e-books and other online material have additional focal points:

- *Hyperlinks.* Clicking on specially formatted words in online text can lead you to additional information. Common hyperlinks include definitions, help, related topics, activities, and web page specifics such as contact information and the privacy policy of the organization or person sponsoring the page.
- *Site index.* The directory gives you a view of the topics included on the website.
- *Menus and tabs.* Navigational tools can help you move to different parts of a document or website, perhaps to see the goals of the site.
- *Multimedia.* Video, interactive features, sounds, and action can enhance your learning experience. Be careful not to confuse advertisements with content.

Active Reading Strategies

An effective reading comprehension technique for online students is based on the acronym READERS, a helpful way to remember the set of actions an active reader takes during and immediately after reading. (See also Key 5.1.)

| **R** Rapidly skim | **E** Evoke memories | **A** Apply critical thinking | **D** Determine main ideas | **E** Engage with others | **R** Review | **S** Summarize |

During Reading				After Reading		
R **Rapidly skim**	**E** **Evoke memories**	**A** **Apply critical thinking**	**D** **Determine main ideas**	**E** **Engage with others**	**R** **Review**	**S** **Summarize**
Skimming the text in an online article or on a website can help you sift through the mountain of information. Prior to reading, get a feel for how the information is organized.	Bringing your prior knowledge to the reading can be very helpful for recalling the information and for understanding it. Ask yourself what you already know about the subject of the reading.	Apply the practices of critical thinking to become a critical reader.	Understanding what you read depends on your ability to recognize the key points in a reading passage. Take notes on these ideas and any supporting evidence by marking and highlighting printed and online material when possible.	Interacting with other people can transform reading from an isolated practice to one that gives you more appreciation of the material.	Review soon after you finish a reading passage to increase your retention of the material.	Summarize what you understand by retelling or rewriting the main points after you finish a reading.

Rapidly Skim

The first step in active reading is to quickly skim the material. In this stage of reading, you can get a grasp of how the reading passage is organized. Scan for the following:

- *Title.* Establishes the topic and often the author's perspective.
- *Headings and subheadings.* Break out important material into bite-size chunks.
- *Introductory and concluding paragraphs.* Generally identify and review the content and main ideas.
- *Tables, charts, graphs, diagrams, photographs, maps, and captions.* Help you quickly assess in a visual manner what the author wants the reader to understand.
- *The table of contents and preface.* Shows the main topics in each chapter and order of coverage. The preface gives an author overview of the book.
- *Chapter elements.* Show the chapter's most important points in chapter introductions or outlines, end-of-chapter summaries, and review questions and exercises
- *Online features.* Gives important information about the material in hyperlinks, a site index, or menus and tabs.

With the amount of information available online, you have to quickly synthesize material, evaluate information, and decide how it meets or does not meet your needs. Because information is not stored or presented in a linear manner online as it is in a textbook, the best way to skim online is to read in an "F" pattern.

Look for menu items across the top and down the left side of a web page—these can help you determine the purpose of the site. Then read the top portion of the text in its entirety to determine the general topic.

Read part of the subsequent section and identify what you can expect to learn from the reading. Assess the difficulty of the text. Will you need to look up vocabulary words you don't know?

Then skim through the rest of the site, looking for headings, multimedia, and all the other elements you might find in printed material or e-books.

Evoke Memories

Caution: The "F" pattern should only be used for skimming and not for actual reading. When you need to comprehend the material, be careful to read it thoroughly.

The next step in active reading is to discover the knowledge you already have. Think about—and summarize in writing if you can—what you already know about the topic, if anything. This prepares you to apply what you know to new material. Bringing up current knowledge is especially important in your major, where courses build on each other and the concepts you learn in a previous class are necessary for a current course.

Ask yourself the following questions about the topic:

- What do I already know about this subject?
- How do I know it?
- What prior knowledge would be useful?
- Is there a way I can gain additional knowledge quickly? (Note that hyperlinks to related information and available videos or stories may provide more information or stimulate your recall of related knowledge.)
- How does the new information fit with my past experience?
- How does what the author is saying relate to any personal insights I have had?
- In what way does this relate to me?

Recalling any prior knowledge or experience you have surrounding the reading material can help you to more quickly and thoroughly comprehend the material.

Apply Critical Thinking

Although textbooks make up a large portion of college reading, your courses will require you to read many other types of materials, such as trade books, journal and newspaper reports, Internet articles, and primary sources (documents created during the time of study, for example, letters, diaries, legal documents, or plays). Being a critical reader—a questioning reader who does not simply accept what you read as truth—is crucial with these types of materials. Even though textbooks are supposed to be as factual and accurate as possible, it can't hurt to keep a critical eye open when reading them as well. A critical reader asks questions in order to evaluate arguments and test the quality of resources.

Ask Questions to Evaluate Arguments

An argument refers to a persuasive case—a set of connected ideas supported by examples—that a writer makes to prove or disprove a point. Many scholarly books and articles, in print form or on the Internet, are organized around particular arguments (look carefully for claims of fact that are actually arguments that need to be supported). Critical readers evaluate arguments and claims to determine whether they are accurate and logical.

It's easy—and common—to accept or reject an argument according to whether it fits with your point of view. If you ask questions, however, you can determine the argument's validity and understand it in greater depth. Evaluating an argument involves looking at several factors.

- *Quality of the evidence.* Do facts, statistics, and other materials support an argument?
- *Suitability of the evidence.* Does the supporting material fit the idea concept?
- *The logical connections.* Does the argument make sense?

When quality evidence combines with sound logic, the argument is solid. Ask the following questions to evaluate the evidence:

- What is the source?
- Is the source reliable and free of bias?
- Who wrote this and with what intent?
- What assumptions underlie this material?
- How does the evidence compare with evidence from other sources?

Ask these questions to determine whether the evidence supports the concept:

- Is there enough evidence?
- Do examples and ideas logically connect to one another?
- Is the evidence convincing? Do the examples build a strong case?
- What different and perhaps opposing arguments seem just as valid?

Approach every argument with a questioning mind. Take time to assess whether you are convinced or have serious questions.

Determine Main Ideas

Understanding what you read depends on your ability to recognize main ideas—the core ideas in a paragraph, segment, or chapter—and link other ideas to them. You are likely to find main ideas at the beginnings or ends of paragraphs.

Ask yourself the following questions about the reading:

- What is the subject?
- How does the subject correspond to the title?
- What are the main points?
- What evidence does the author give?
- Do the author's ideas seem correct?
- What would make a good headline summary of the material?
- Why is the information stated as it is?
- Is the author trying to persuade the reader?

Take notes on the main ideas and supporting evidence. You can also mark up and highlight printed text. Many e-book reader programs allow you to take notes onscreen or highlight portions of the material. In some cases, you can also cut and paste important information from electronic documents into a word processing program (being sure to copy into your notes the web citation information or print the first page of the web material so you have the source to refer to when documentation is needed). Sometimes you may want to print out online reading material to take notes or to read or study at a time or place that electronic access may not be available to you.

As you read, practice the "look-away method." Periodically look away from the text, summarize the section you have just read, and ask yourself a question about the material. If you cannot say it or write the answer, then you may not understand the main ideas. Go back and reread the section and try again.

After you identify the main ideas in a passage, see whether you can make predictions about what is to come. Can you identify a pattern in the reading?

Engage with Others

By talking and writing about reading, you can uncover how others process information and find meaning. Interacting with your classmates can transform reading from an isolated practice to one that gives you more enthusiasm and appreciation of the material.

You may have the opportunity to do this as part of a required online discussion assignment. If not, you can use another online forum, such as the chat room in your course or blogs and online journals. Often, there are places for comments for material found on websites. Look at comments, give opinions, vote online if you can, or discuss the material with a partner or group. Talking to friends and family as well about the reading can help you understand and make better connections to the material, improving the likelihood that it will be retained in your long-term memory.

Before discussing the reading with others, though, set aside a little time just to reflect on the material. Then discuss the concepts. After the discussion, determine whether your interpretation of the material changed at all.

Watch your speed. When people read on a screen they tend to stop after skimming and only focus on headings and subheadings, key words, bullet points, and color. Make sure you slow down and focus in the same way you would when reading printed material.

Review

Studies show that between 40 and 50 percent of what we read is lost within 15 minutes of reading it. After spending so much time going through material, it seems counterproductive to lose it. Review soon after you finish a reading passage, which can increase your retention of the material up to 80 percent. Reviewing both immediately and periodically in the days and weeks after you read will help you learn new material. If you never refer to the reading again, you will probably forget almost everything.

Try these reviewing strategies and use what works best:

- Reread your notes and then summarize them from memory.
- Make an outline of key ideas or related concepts and identify relationships.
- Make flash cards with words or concepts on one side and definitions, examples, or other related information on the other. Test yourself.
- Quiz yourself on the material you read.

Refreshing your knowledge is easier and faster than learning it the first time. Make a weekly review schedule and stick to it until you're sure you know everything.

Summarize

Do a short free-write after you are done reading—in other words, describe what you read and how you felt about it, writing for your eyes only. What did you connect with?

Why? What troubled you? Did you relate to the reading? If so, why? If not, what kind of plan can you think of when you sit back down to continue working through it?

Then, summarize what you understand by retelling, or rewriting, the main points. Ask yourself questions like the following:

- What have I learned?
- Given what I know about the subject, are the main points correct?
- What causes me to doubt the main points?
- If I could speak to the author, what questions would I ask or what criticism would I offer?

Online Reading Challenges

Complex Material

Understanding sentence structure is quite important, especially when reading challenging college-level material online. Better readers understand the basic rules of grammar and sentence structure. Primarily, they are able to separate a subject phrase from a predicate, or verb, phrase in a sentence. This "phrase-cutting" strategy was observed in print material as early as A.D. 400, when Saint Jerome first noticed that some scribes had placed phrases on separate lines as a way to help poor readers read the text aloud.

For complicated material, you can follow this same strategy if you can cut and paste the material into a word processing program. From there, you can manipulate the text and break large, complex material down into shorter chunks. Divide the text into phrases or thematic segments like paragraphs or subheadings to better enable you to sift through it.

Eyestrain

Online reading has unique challenges. Not only do you have to locate information quickly and accurately, but you have to do this while looking at a computer screen for hours at a time. The reading material is very visually intensive, and you may experience eyestrain. The stationary screens of desktop and laptop computers lend themselves to static and tiring reading positions. In addition, most applications and text formats are designed for the word processors and Web browsers, so their resolution is lower than desired for minimizing eye strain.

CREATE

Create a Summary

Free-write what you have learned about so far in this chapter. Summarize the main points in your own words.

Find a website with one or two pages of higher-level material that you are able to copy and paste into a Word document. Copy the same material into two documents. In one of the documents, insert extra spaces and divisions between paragraphs. In the other document, do not make any changes. First, read the unchanged document. Note the time it takes you to get through the page and any reading challenges you face. Next, read the document with extra spaces. As you read using the READERS strategy, insert additional spaces when you find a division between ideas or phrases. Which reading experience is more effective and enjoyable? What other strategies can you implement to make reading complex material easier?

When you spend a lot of time at the computer, be sure to take frequent short breaks, look away from the screen, close your eyes, or focus on something else across the room.

Expand or maximize the window so it fills the entire screen. This will make reading easier. Also, make the print larger so you are not hunched over the computer or straining to see what's on the screen.

Extensive practice is an essential part of learning any skill, including reading. No one can learn to read complicated material by trying once or twice. Effective practice requires active, focused, repeated effort over time. Practice being an active reader whenever you get the opportunity.

Reading Strategies for Different Learning Styles

Use your strengths to improve your reading comprehension. Recall your learning style. Can you apply any additional suggestions from previous discussions of these factors here? See Key 5.2 for more ideas.

At this point in the term you undoubtedly have some reading to do. Put what you have learned in this chapter to use in becoming a more strategic and critical reader. Practice these skills whenever you get a chance. As you have learned, reading skills are *very* important for your future career success.

The number one reason patients visit eye doctors is because of computer strain. The U.S. Occupational Safety and Health Administration has issued guidelines to reduce eyestrain from computer display use in the workplace. For more information on the guidelines, go to www.osha.gov/SLTC/etools/computerworkstations/components_monitors.html

Look to continually challenge yourself. Stretch beyond your current reading level and make yourself work at understanding.

ONLINE OUTLOOK

PETER
Online reader
Age 40

CHALLENGE
Reading online

I am one of those people who like to read on the computer. For some reason, I have always found the light that comes off the computer screen stimulating. I like to read from the computer when I can. Although I do occasionally suffer from eyestrain, it seems to have lessened the more time I spend at my computer.

For months after I first began working on computers every day, all day, I found sunlight too strong. I would scrunch my eyelids and my eyes would water every lunchtime.

I do print out many documents still and when I can, I copy and paste poorly designed website material into Word. Then, I can change the color and fonts to make it easier to read.

Intelligence		Strategies
Verbal-Linguistic		Use text-to-speech software to have the text selection read aloud to you as you read it. Sound out difficult words, and read difficult passages aloud. Try guessing word meanings based on what you read before and after difficult vocabulary. Then, look the words up in a dictionary. Take advantage of online dictionaries, audio guides to word pronunciation, and the ability to modify the presentation of online text to one which you can easily read. Using a word processor, turn digital text into an outline or cut and paste examples that support the main points of the reading. Use highlight features of any e-books to highlight important sections. Use other software programs, such as PowerPoint or website design programs, to summarize readings.
Logical-Mathematical		Logically connect what you are reading with what you already know. Draw charts and graphs showing relationships. Take notes in a spreadsheet program that can help you identify similarities and differences and causes and effects. Use a word processing, website design, or drawing program to cut and paste the main ideas and supporting information, and make connections between them. Rearrange or add other ideas to make additional connections.
Bodily-Kinesthetic		Print out text and highlight important parts of the reading. After reading, go on a walk while you are summarizing the material aloud.
Visual-Spatial		Make use of any visuals, such as pictures, charts, and diagrams provided, to help you assess your prior knowledge, inspire questions, and determine the main ideas of the reading. Consider other visuals you could add that could help explain the concepts. Create a simple video by drawing pictures representing the main points of the reading on small pieces of paper and then flipping through them while recording. Take pictures of charts and diagrams and assemble the images in a PowerPoint type presentation or animation program. Visualize or imagine a "word picture" that will help you relate your experience with the reading. Draw a word-map to understand the relationships of concepts to a key word. Make use of site maps to help tell you where particular sections or pages are found within the site.

Intelligence	Strategies
Interpersonal	Consult with the professor, a tutor, an academic advisor, a classmate, a study group, or other resource if you have difficulty comprehending what you are reading.
	Collaborate with others, sharing outlines and understandings of the meaning, brainstorming relationships to other ideas, etc.
	Set up wikis for collaborative reading, where each person can share their background knowledge before reading, their summaries, and their opinions after reading.
Intrapersonal	Keep your mind on the connected thought as you read.
	Apply the concepts to your own life.
	Browse the online library collection for related ideas.
	As you read, consider different outcomes. Predict what the author will say.
	Practice reading aloud for continuity and smoothness.
Musical	Read aloud, creating a rhythm, pace and cadence that includes pauses.
	Use expressive tones that represent the action or emotion.
	Consider what musical score would go along with the text presentation.
	Write songs that summarize the material.
Naturalistic	Cut and paste parts of the text in a word processing program, grouping common elements together.
	Organize your reading materials and notes into relevant groupings.
	Some web pages are also now being encoded with information to categorize and structure their information, with the goal of creating a "semantic web" that can give readers new power to access, organize, and analyze digital information. Research more about this as it becomes further developed.

Understand Printed Text Using SQ3R

One of the most successful comprehension techniques for college students was first developed by Francis Pleasant Robinson in 1946. SQ3R, an acronym for survey, question, read, recite, and review, is a comprehension tool for the active thinker designed for use with printed textbooks.

Step 1: Survey

The first stage of SQ3R, surveying, involves previewing, or prereading, your assignment. As noted in our discussion of the first item of READERS, most textbooks include elements that provide a big picture overview of the main ideas and themes, including contents, chapter outlines and headings, and review questions.

Step 2: Question

The next step is to ask questions about your assignment. Before you begin reading, think about—and summarize in writing if you can—what you already know about the topic, if anything. Next, use a questioning process to focus on what you are still uncertain about, which can lead you to discover knowledge on your own, making an investment in the material and in your own memory.

Step 3: The Three Rs: Read, Recite, Review

Read

Your text survey and questions give you a starting point for reading, the first R in SQ3R. Retaining what you read requires an active approach:

Understand the key points of your survey. Pay special attention to points raised in headings, in boldface type, in chapter objectives and summary, and so on.

Focus on your questions. Read the material with the purpose of answering each question. Write down or highlight ideas and examples that relate to your questions.

Look for the main idea. Understanding what you read depends on your ability to recognize main ideas—the core ideas in a paragraph, segment, or chapter—and link other ideas to them. You are likely to find main ideas at the beginning or end of a paragraph.

Mark up your text. Write notes in the margins or on separate paper, circle main ideas, or highlight key supporting details to focus on what's important. These cues will boost memory and help you study for exams. The tips on the next page show a technique for taking marginal notes right on the pages of your text.

PRACTICE & plan apply

How would you assess your reading now in terms of speed and comprehension? Are you satisfied with your ability? Would you like to improve?

PLAN

Pretend that you have been asked to teach a junior high school class how to improve their reading comprehension and speed for both textbooks and online research. The goal of the talk is not only to motivate students to develop good habits but also to provide concrete tips they can use. Identify at least three objective actions the students can take or behaviors they can change to improve reading speed and comprehension.

- Use pencil so you can erase comments or questions that are answered later as you review.
- Write your questions in the margins next to text headings.
- Mark critical sections with marginal notations such as: "Def." for definition, "E.g." for helpful example, "Concept" for an important concept, and so on.
- Write notes at the bottom of the page connecting the text to what you learned in class or in research. You can also attach adhesive notes with your comments.
- Highlight your text. Highlighting involves the use of special markers or regular pens or pencils to flag important passages. Use these tips to make highlighting a true learning tool.
- Develop a system and stick to it. For example, use your creative intelligence to decide whether to use different colored markers for different elements, brackets for long passages, or pencil underlining. Make a key that identifies each notation.
- Consider using a regular pencil or pen instead of a highlighter pen. The copy will be cleaner and look more like a textbook than a coloring book.
- Read an entire paragraph before you begin to highlight, and don't start until you have a sense of what is important. Only then put pencil or highlighter to paper as you pick out key terms, phrases, and ideas.
- Avoid overmarking. A phrase or two in any paragraph is usually enough. Enclose long passages with brackets rather than marking every line. Avoid underlining entire sentences, when possible. The less color the better.
- Highlight supporting evidence. Mark examples that explain important ideas.

Recite

Once you finish reading a topic, stop and answer the questions you raised in the second stage of SQ3R. Even if you have already done this during the reading phase, do it again now—with the purpose of learning and committing the material to memory.

Try reciting each answer aloud, silently speaking the answers to yourself, "teaching" the answers to another person, or writing them down. Consider your learning style as you find what works best. Whatever your method, make sure you know how ideas connect to one another and to the general concept.

Review

Reviewing what you read in the days and weeks after will help you learn the material.

Reading Speed

1. _____

2. _____

3. _____

Reading Comprehension

1. _____

2. _____

3. _____

APPLY

Can you apply the strategies to your own reading? How would you evaluate the success of developing new reading habits?

NOTE-TAKING
for Online Courses

Compressing Information

6

BASIC NOTE-TAKING TECHNIQUES

- Deciding What to Record
- Deciding Where to Keep Notes

NOTE-TAKING SITUATIONS

- Note-Taking While Reading
- Note-Taking for Multimedia Presentations
- Collaborative Note-Taking

NOTE-TAKING STRATEGIES

- Outlining
- T-Format (Cornell System)
- Think Links
- Strategies for Different Learning Styles

ASK YOURSELF

Would you consider yourself a successful note-taker? How does taking notes differ depending on whether you are reading or watching a video lecture?

IN THIS CHAPTER

you'll explore answers to the following questions:

- How can you improve your note-taking abilities?
- What are useful strategies for taking notes while reading?
- What are useful strategies for taking notes from multimedia?
- What are some different note-taking systems?

Analyze

Taking a self-assessment can help you think more deeply about your own skills and preferences. Consider the questions in this assessment and your responses. What information does this quiz provide about yourself that you can use to develop or improve important skills?

Rate Yourself as an Active Student

For each statement, circle the number that feels right to you, from 1 for "not true for me" to 5 for "very true for me."

▶ If I am using new technology, I like to practice it to make sure I'm comfortable before I need it.   1   2   3   4   5

▶ I have a place to take notes that is convenient and readily accessible when needed.   1   2   3   4   5

▶ I try to stay focused from beginning to end when I watch a video on an important subject.   1   2   3   4   5

▶ I have a plan for "capturing" tough ideas I didn't initially grasp.   1   2   3   4   5

▶ I have common abbreviations that I use for taking notes.   1   2   3   4   5

▶ I try to minimize internal and external distractions when I'm studying.   1   2   3   4   5

▶ I am open to learning about different note-taking systems.   1   2   3   4   5

▶ Taking notes helps me to retain the information better.   1   2   3   4   5

▶ I use different note-taking strategies in class depending on the situation.   1   2   3   4   5

▶ I review and revise my notes on the same day I take them.   1   2   3   4   5

Now total your scores.   _____

If your total ranges from 38–50, you consider your note-taking skills to be strong. You may find that taking notes from multimedia sources is different from note-taking during reading, however. Read through the strategies in this chapter and practice on those you feel you can improve.

If your total ranges from 24–37, you consider your note-taking skills to be average. You may want to improve in one or two situations. Perhaps you can take excellent notes from reading but struggle with note-taking from a video source, or vice versa. Find your challenge, use the strategies for your learning style, and improve these skills now to benefit your future education and career endeavors.

If your total ranges from 10–23, you consider your note-taking skills to be weak. This chapter can help you develop strategies for taking notes in several situations, from online and print reading material and from video lectures and other multimedia sources. Practice the techniques as often as possible, and you will likely also find that your critical thinking skills improve as well.

Analyze: How can you use technology to take notes? What are the pitfalls?

One of the stumbling blocks most online students face is taking—and organizing—good notes. The goal of note-taking is to record a condensed version of important points and supporting information. Like reading, note-taking is a skill that can be learned and refined. Although it takes some practice, note-taking doesn't have to be a hassle. In fact, when you become accustomed to taking good notes, they'll come easier every time.

There are many benefits to taking notes. As you go through the process, you contemplate what you are learning, organize the points, summarize, make connections, prioritize knowledge, and synthesize ideas. In doing so, you develop your own method for understanding the core content, and you achieve deeper learning.

Notes also provide a record of information that can quickly refresh your memory or help you navigate open book exams. In your career, there will likely be many meetings, readings, lectures, or research opportunities when you will need to determine the most important points, condense them, and combine ideas. Learning good note-taking skills now will be quite valuable to your future.

Technology allows for new methods of both content delivery and note-taking. In your online course, you may have readings, including your texts, websites, content presentations, and articles, as well as video lectures, podcasts, and interactive media. You can take notes electronically using online text annotation, digital notes, copy and paste features, and collaborative note sharing. You can take notes on your desktop or laptop computer or via a PDA or smartphone.

In this chapter, you will learn how to take notes while reading printed and online material, from video lectures, and while engaging with more interactive resources. There are several ways to take notes, and you can choose among them to find what works best for you.

Researchers have found that if important information is contained in notes, it has a 34 percent chance of being remembered. Information not found in notes only has a 5 percent chance of being remembered.*

Basic Note-Taking
Techniques

Deciding What to Record

The first step, no matter what note-taking system you use, is to identify which item to record. You don't want to write down everything said or read verbatim, of course, but how much is enough? How much is too much?

Good notes will include the key points. Once you have determined the main topic, note it with emphasis. Then you can start looking for the subtopics, which should be well marked and underlined in your notes. Identifying key words, as shown in Key 6.1, can give you a hint as to the main focus. When you read or hear definitions or examples, take note! Something important is under discussion. Also be sure to note your ongoing questions.

*Longman, D., & Atkinson, R. (1999). *College Learning and Study Skills*. Belmont, CA: Wadsworth/Thomson Learning.

Signals Pointing to Key Concepts

A key point to remember . . .

Point 1, point 2, etc. . . .

The impact of this was . . .

The critical stages in the process are . . .

Signals Pointing to Differences

On the contrary, . . .

On the other hand, . . .

In contrast, . . .

However, . . .

Signals of Support

A perfect example . . .

Specifically, . . .

For instance, . . .

Similarly, . . .

Signals That Summarize

From this you have learned . . .

In conclusion, . . .

As a result, . . .

Finally, . . .

- *Definitions.* Note any new vocabulary words, names, events, dates, steps, or directions; or any new procedure that is explained or any new concept.

- *Examples.* Mark the cases that explain and support the important ideas. You might try using more than one highlighter color to differentiate definitions or ideas from examples.

- *Questions.* Because online courses sometimes won't offer immediate opportunities for questions while engaging with the material, it is easy to forget or ignore them. Write down any questions you think of while watching a video lecture or reading course material. Try to answer these questions yourself or see whether the reading or lecture provides answers as you continue. Keep a running list of questions to ask your instructor during a chat session or by e-mail.

Use Shortcuts

Consider the following sentence:

> Julie has a question about problem number one and would like an answer.

If you took notes using the following characters, you can condense this sentence from 58 characters to 26:

> J has ? Re: prob 1 & wants answer.

Choose your own symbols and abbreviations to use. The key is to break larger words down into shortened versions so you can write faster. You can use instant and text messaging symbols to record important ideas. To avoid forgetting what your shorthand means, review your notes while your symbols are fresh. If you are confused, spell out words as you review. Key 6.2 shows popular shorthand notations; you can find more on the Internet.

Deciding Where to Keep Your Notes

You may take handwritten notes or type your notes into a word processor or note-taking program. Use a system that is easy and convenient for you.

Be cautious when copying and pasting material as part of note-taking. It is easy to take wordier notes, recording all words associated with an idea, no matter how important. You may not pay attention to critical details or receive the same retention benefits from note-taking as students who create their own notes. If you do copy and paste, summarize the section in your own words.

w/, w/o	with, without	Cf	compare, in comparison to
ur	you are	Ff	following
→	means; resulting in	Q	question
←	as a result of	gr8	great
↑	increasing	Pov	point of view
↓	decreasing	<	less than
∴	therefore	>	more than
b/c	because	=	equals
≈	approximately	b&f	back and forth
+ *or* &	and	Δ	change
Y	why	2	to; two; too
no. *or* #	number	Afap	as far as possible
i.e.	that is,	e.g.	for example
cos	change of subject	c/o	care of
Ng	no good	lb	pound
POTUS	president of the United States	hx	history

When taking notes in an online course, you may be able to use a notes feature within the online course management system. Most likely, however, if you do this, you will only be able to access your notes while you are logged in.

To review your notes at any time, you can use a word processing program, such as Microsoft Word. By setting up two documents next to each other on the screen, you can toggle between the document you are reading and the one on which you are taking notes.

There are hundreds of Web applications for keeping notes (such as GradeGuru, WiseCampus, and Sharenotes) as well that enable you to have access anywhere you have an Internet connection. Many students use wikis to keep notes throughout their school career.

Other basic techniques for notes are described in Key 6.3.

Wikis are free content-sharing websites that can be searched. Using wikis gives you the ability to access notes taken years earlier if necessary. Wikis can link to other pages and other sites on the Web, bringing new bodies of information together in one place.

CREATE

Abbreviations

Create abbreviations for at least twenty common terms in your program.

Write legibly if taking handwritten notes. If you can't read your own notes a few days afterward, they are of little use. The best place to keep handwritten notes is in a loose-leaf notebook. Use dividers to separate the different classes you take.

Review your notes within 24 hours of first studying the material. When reviewing, make sure that you understand what your abbreviated words mean and clarify everything while it is still fresh in your mind. If there are points that need further research, do so at once.

Read a little more. It's worth it to do a little extra reading because your study notes will have more meaning if you take it upon yourself to read more on the subject.

Date and label your notes. Writing the date and labeling the subject of your class on all your notes is a great habit to get into.

Revise and synthesize your notes. It can be very helpful to synthesize your notes from all sources on a regular basis, such as once a week. If you take notes from the course presentation, cross-reference those with your notes from the text and readings, videos, podcasts, and other material. Recopying and synthesizing your notes will give you a complete set of notes to review when you are getting ready for the exams, assignments, and projects. The process of recopying your notes also helps cement the material into your long-term memory.

Note-Taking
Situations

Online programs can offer a variety of note-taking opportunities, including the textbook, web pages, journal articles, and other printed material. Whether for research projects or as part of assigned coverage, you may take notes when watching videos, listening to podcasts, or while interacting with other multimedia offerings in your course. You may then need to synthesize all of your notes.

Note-Taking While Reading

You can take notes on a variety of reading sources, both printed and online. Don't be afraid to highlight your printed textbooks and make notes in the margins. Many online e-book readers allow you to take notes using annotation and highlighting tools. If you are unable to take notes on the electronic version, you may be able to copy and paste the reading into a word processing program where you can take notes or you may choose to print out copies of online articles and text pages that you are not able to annotate. The following tips offer helpful suggestions for taking notes while reading:

1. *Stop occasionally.* Take in what you are reading and use your critical thinking and reading skills. Recall some of the questions about the text you can ask:
   - What is the point of this article?
   - Are the author's arguments convincing?
   - Who did the author write this piece for?
   - When was this information written and when was it published?
2. *Mark up your text.* Take notes in the margins and highlight main ideas and key supporting details to focus on what's important. Use different colors for each if your note-taking system allows you to do so. Different techniques can facilitate taking marginal notes right on the pages of your text:
   - Write any questions next to text headings.
   - Mark critical sections with marginal notations such as: "Def." for definition, "E.g." for helpful example, "Concept" for an important concept, and so on.

- Write notes at the bottom of the page connecting the text to what you have learned in other places.

3. *Highlight your text.* Use a special pen or software feature to flag important passages. When used correctly, highlighting is an essential learning technique. Following a few simple tips can make highlighting a true learning tool:

   - Develop a system and stick to it. For example, use different colors or methods of underlining for different elements like main ideas, supporting evidence, or key terms. Whatever your system, be consistent.
   - Read an entire paragraph before you begin to highlight, and don't start until you have a sense of what is important. Only highlight as you pick out key terms, phrases, and ideas.
   - Avoid overmarking. A phrase or two in any paragraph is usually enough. Avoid underlining entire sentences, when possible. The less color the better.

Consider taking notes on index cards or in Microsoft PowerPoint. You can sort, edit, and arrange index cards or PowerPoint slides to suit your particular study needs. Use the cards for study and review or to help organize information for papers, reports, or projects.

Note-Taking for Multimedia Presentations

Watching a video lecture or Web conference, whether live or prerecorded, can make it possible to see and hear an instructor or expert source as though you were attending a lecture in real life.

When taking notes from a live Web conference, lecture, news event, or other presentation, it is very helpful to be comfortable with the technology before it begins. Log in a few minutes early so that if you encounter any technical problems, you have time to troubleshoot or ask for help.

Consider the following strategies when taking notes from multimedia sources:

- *Review any previous notes and readings.* Looking over earlier material can provide context for new information.

- *Anticipate what is coming.* Before the lecture, write down a predicted outline of the topic.

- *Take down the initial details.* Date the session, and title the notes with the subject of the lecture or presentation. Write out the full name of the person lecturing or being interviewed and/or the channel you're watching or listening to.

- *Identify the main points.* As you listen to the lecture, remind yourself to ask questions. "What is the point?" "What am I learning?" "What is this story an illustration of?" "What is this example demonstrating?" Skip lines after crucial points and use bullets (like those used in this list) for supporting information.

ONLINE OUTLOOK

SARA
Age 27

CHALLENGE
Taking notes

One of the things that helped me the most with taking notes was to look at how my friends did it. One friend, in particular, was a master at taking notes from the text.

He marked up every page without fear! He circled words; he wrote his own headings in the margins; he used arrows to connect paragraphs or ideas; he underlined key passages.

It was a marvel to me! I learned a lot from looking at how he did it.

Active Listening

You may not get many opportunities in an online course to practice valuable listening skills, but watching video lectures provides a chance to improve. Listening isn't always easy and it isn't always comfortable. Take the words of Robert Frost for instance: "Education is the ability to listen to almost anything without losing your temper or your self-confidence." Keeping an open, awake, and engaged mind takes practice, but when excellent listening becomes second nature, you'll thank yourself for the work it took.

Strategies for listening actively to speakers include the following:

- Get enough sleep to stay alert and eat enough so you're not hungry—or have small snacks nearby.
- Put your worries aside. If you can't, take a break if possible and come back to the lecture refocused.
- Start with a productive mindset. If the material is difficult, that's all the more reason to pay attention.
- Concentrate. Work to take in the whole message so you will be able to read over your notes later and think critically about what is important. Making connections between ideas can alleviate the difficulty of the material in some cases—or boredom if you're familiar with the concepts.
- If you experience a listening lapse, get back into the lecture quickly instead of worrying about what you missed. After class, look at a classmate's notes to fill in the gaps.
- Be aware. Pay attention to verbal signposts—words or phrases that call attention to what comes next, help organize information, connect ideas, or indicate what is important and what is not. See Key 6.1 for examples.
- Be careful not to rush to judgment. Know that you can't hear others—and therefore can't learn anything—if you are filled with preconceived notions about them and their ideas.

- *Record your own responses.* Answer the instructor's questions, even if you don't voice your response. Distinguish between what is said and your commentary. You might put your personal thoughts, questions, and commentary in brackets.

- *Summarize.* Free-write a one page summary of the lecture or presentation shortly after watching the lecture. Summarize important points in your own words. Highlight any actions that you need to take.

- *Share notes.* If you can find someone else who attended the lecture or presentation, watched the same media program, or read the same material, discuss it with each other.

Collaborative Note-Taking

Students can work together to create comprehensive notes using several note-taking approaches including discussion boards, blogs, social networking sites, instant messaging, chat, wikis, public pages, bulletin boards, and other sources.

Collaborative note-taking, which is growing in popularity, offers several benefits. In addition to encouraging deeper learning, it allows social learning to take place. It reinforces knowledge and provides multiple perspectives while requiring critical thinking skills.

However, there are also some drawbacks. Other students' notes can often be unreliable and inaccurate from lack of skill or effort. Moreover, students learn better when they are more involved in the learning process. Be careful not to let note sharing replace note-taking; students who become passive will miss out on the benefits of taking notes in much the same way as someone who goes to the gym only to watch others exercise. The true value of notes is to provide critical anchor points to let the material sink in.

Linear learners will appreciate note-taking methods specifically designed for them, including the T-format, outlining, and tabular methods, whereas nonlinear and visual learners may appreciate the mapping technique.

Note-Taking Formats

Now that you have an idea how to take great notes, you'll need a personalized method for taking them. As you read about the following systems, keep certain questions in mind:

- What type of media would this system be best suited for? Why?
- How could I make use of this system?
- Which system seems most comfortable to me?
- What system might be most compatible with my learning style? Why?

Though some note-taking systems may be better suited for different purposes, you can pick and choose depending on your preference. See Key 6.4 for examples.

Outlining

Many students use informal outlines for in-class note-taking. An outline is a structure to help organize information from lectures and readings. It can also be a way to arrange your own thoughts. It generally takes the following form, though you may use variations for your note-taking purposes:

KEY 6.4	Note-Taking Techniques by Purpose
Primary Note-Taking Purpose	**Primary Note-Taking Techniques**
Brainstorm	Think links, journaling
Explore ideas and gather more information	Tabular, journaling, T-format
Synthesize ideas	T-format, think links
Focus on a topic's details	Index cards, outlining
Present information	Outlining, index cards

    I. First main idea
        A. First subdivision of main idea
            i. First reason or example
            ii. Second reason or example
                1. first supporting detail
                2. second supporting detail
        B. Second subdivision of main idea
    II. Second main idea

The following structure of an informal outline helps a student take notes on the topic of tropical rain forests.

Tropical Rain Forests*

What are tropical rain forests?
    —Areas in S. America and Africa, along equator
    —Average temperatures between 25° and 30°C (77°–86°F)
    —Average annual rainfalls between 250 to 400 centimeters (100 to 160 inches)
    —Conditions combine to create the Earth's richest, most biodiverse ecosystem

A biodiverse ecosystem has a great number of organisms co-existing within a defined area.

*Audesirk, T., Audesirk, G., & Byers, B. E. (2000). *Life on Earth* (2nd ed.). Upper Saddle River, NJ: Prentice Hall.

Examples of rainforest biodiversity

—2½ acres in the Amazon rainforest has 283 species of trees

—3-square-mile section of Peruvian rain forest has more than 1,300 butterfly species and 600 bird species.

Compare this biodiversity to that in the entire U.S.

—400 butterfly species and 700 bird species

T-Format (Cornell System)

If you lack sufficient experience in taking notes, begin by using some form of double-entry system in order to gain practice in recording both content and your personal response. This format, which is shown in Key 6.5, is referred to as the T-format.

KEY 6.5   T-Format

The Question or Topic	
Content Summary (what it says)	Personal response
	Tie to previous content
	Why this is enlightening
	Why this is important
	A new question generated

The Cornell System is an advanced T-format. Divide the page into three parts, as in Key 6.6. The narrower left side is used later to synthesize main ideas, with the wider right side reserved for gathering details. The bottom area is to summarize what the notes mean as well as your judgment on the quality of information along with any additional support evidence or clarification needed.

This system is similar to a box score for an athletic event, which might include the most important players, plays, scoring events, and team totals. Similarly, you can keep track of the most important information from the lecture, presentation, interview, or reading using this method.

As notes are taken using the Cornell system, leave space between details, usually one inch for every two inches of notes taken. This allows for clearer notes and room to interject related information presented later.

If the presentation is interactive and you're able to ask questions, you can note the areas you would like to ask about with a question mark and later fill in the responses.

Think Links

A think link, also referred to as a "mind map" or "word web," uses shapes and lines to link ideas to supporting details. The visual design makes the connections easy to see, and shapes and pictures extend the material beyond words. This can help illustrate ideas, concepts, and relationships as you take notes.

ONLINE app

To create a think link, start by circling or boxing your topic in the middle of the paper. Next draw a line from the topic and write the name of one major idea at the end of the line. Circle that idea. Then jot down specific facts related to the idea, linking them to the idea with lines. Continue the process, connecting thoughts to one another with circles, lines, and words. The image in Key 6.7, a think link on the sociological concept stratification, follows this structure.

Cornell System

Subject:

Date:

Main idea	Details
Inferences	
New Questions	

Summary

Include here a brief abstract of meaning to you and your judgment on the quality of information as well as additional support evidence or clarification needed.

KEY 6.7   **Use a Think Link to Connect Ideas Visually**

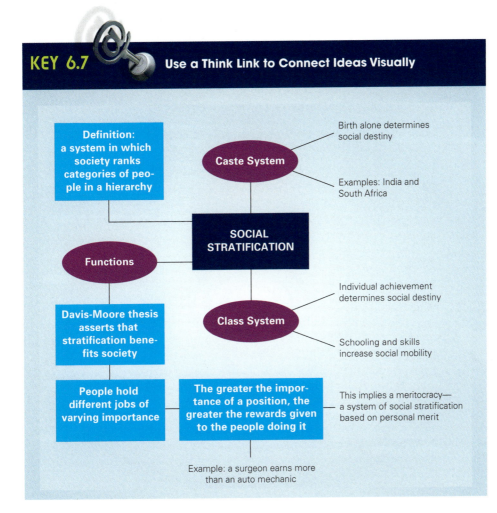

Definition: a system in which society ranks categories of people in a hierarchy

Caste System
- Birth alone determines social destiny
- Examples: India and South Africa

SOCIAL STRATIFICATION

Functions

Davis-Moore thesis asserts that stratification benefits society

Class System
- Individual achievement determines social destiny
- Schooling and skills increase social mobility

People hold different jobs of varying importance

The greater the importance of a position, the greater the rewards given to the people doing it

This implies a meritocracy—a system of social stratification based on personal merit

Example: a surgeon earns more than an auto mechanic

Note-Taking Strategies for Different Learning Styles

Active, engaged note-taking is a skill that extends far beyond the classroom. Conquering this skill now while in college will not only help your academic career but will also have an impact on your value as an employee. See Key 6.8 for examples.

KEY 6.8 — Note-Taking Strategies for Different Learning Styles

Intelligence	Strategies
Verbal-Linguistic	Retype class notes in an alternate note-taking format to see connections more clearly. Using a word processor, turn digital text into an outline or cut and paste examples that support the main points of the reading. Use highlight features of any e-books to highlight important sections.
Logical-Mathematical	Organize information along a continuum. Visualize a group of four ideas and see how they relate to each other. Use a spreadsheet program to take notes and identify any common features or themes across different subjects. Use timelines for note-taking, to help identify important events and processes.
Bodily-Kinesthetic	Print out notes and use colored highlighters. Use note cards to arrange notes in different orders and sequences. Take notes by using a voice memo feature while listening to the course podcast and walking or jogging. After reading or watching a video presentation, go on a walk while you are summarizing and recording your notes.
Visual-Spatial	To take notes electronically, open a word processing or note-taking program or paint or drawing program in a corner of your computer. Use a Venn Diagram (overlapping circles) to compare and contrast different ideas, texts, authors, characters, eras—and to identify the ways in which they are similar and different. Take notes in a generic web page template. It works very well as a visual organizing device. Draw a word-map to understand the relationships of concepts to a key word. Make use of site maps to help tell you where particular sections or pages are found within the site.
Interpersonal	Discuss the reading with other students. Open a thread in the discussion board or student chat area and ask others to post what they thought of certain reading or online presentation. Collaborate with others, sharing notes. Use wikis when organizing study groups. Divide a topic up into pieces for each person. As you work, link to your co-students' pages, and vice versa. As new material is covered, you can go back and edit each other's pages or correct each other's mistakes. Exchange notes with a buddy and make up a test for each other from the other's notes.

Intelligence		Strategies
Intrapersonal		Lecture to the wall. After a class, take your notes and literally face the wall and teach the notes to it.
		When reviewing your notes, identify distinct scenes or moments in your notes and explain what is happening and why it is important.
		Quiz yourself from your notes.
Musical		Write songs that summarize your notes.
		Use all your senses to help you see what the author is writing, to hear what the language sounds like.
Naturalistic		Organize your notes into a hierarchy.
		Use a Venn Diagram (overlapping circles) as a different way to look at a subject and make connections.
		Make inferences in your notes about how one event relates to another, how one event inspired or lead to another.
		Bring your text, lecture notes, and other pertinent information to an outdoor spot that inspires you and helps you to feel confident. Review your material there.

PRACTICE & plan apply

Critical reading is the first step in taking good notes from online text sources. The purpose of this writing assignment is to help you learn how to take better notes.

1. Find an editorial from a respected news source online.
2. Identify the article by title, publication, date, and author.
3. In a sentence or two, summarize the author's position.

PLAN

Before taking notes, identify the conclusion and the evidence supporting the position. Identify any bias or challenge to the credibility of the information.

Conclusion:

Supporting Evidence:

Credibility Challenges:

APPLY

Take notes on the argument the author makes using one of the note-taking systems. Then try another note-taking system with the same article. Which works best for you? Why?

7 ONLINE Course Assignments and Test-Taking

Zooming In

UNDERSTANDING ASSIGNMENTS

- Before You Begin
- Approaching Different Types of Assignments
- ANSWER the Question

CHARACTERISTICS OF EFFECTIVE WRITING

- Clear Topic
- Good Organization
- Writer's Own Material and Voice
- Sentence Variety
- Conciseness
- Correct Grammar and Punctuation
- Good Design

APPLYING STRATEGIES FOR DIFFERENT LEARNING STYLES

ASK YOURSELF

How developed are your writing skills? Can you communicate your thoughts both informally and formally in writing? How does the tone of your writing change depending on the purpose?

IN THIS CHAPTER

you'll explore answers to the following questions:

- How can you tackle most assignments?
- What are the characteristics of effective writing?
- How can you approach the different types of assignments in an online course?

Analyze

Taking a self-assessment can help you think more deeply about your own skills and preferences. Consider the questions in this assessment and your responses. What information does this quiz provide about yourself that you can use to develop or improve important skills?

Rate Yourself as a Writer

For each statement, circle the number that feels right to you, from 1 for "not true for me" to 5 for "very true for me."

▶ I have a system for making sure I answer every assignment question effectively.   1 2 3 4 5

▶ I use different writing styles for different types of writing assignments.   1 2 3 4 5

▶ I make sure I cite every source.   1 2 3 4 5

▶ I proofread my writing assignments at least a couple of times before I submit them.   1 2 3 4 5

▶ I know how to give and receive feedback on writing assignments.   1 2 3 4 5

▶ I avoid using informal language in written assignments.   1 2 3 4 5

▶ I know how to approach the different types of writing required for online courses.   1 2 3 4 5

▶ I know how to write a topic sentence.   1 2 3 4 5

▶ I understand that all writing assignment submissions should be organized   1 2 3 4 5

▶ I have a strategy for taking online tests.   1 2 3 4 5

Now total your scores.   _____

If your total ranges from 38–50, you consider your writing skills to be strong. This is going to be a great asset in your online education because you will write often—for most of your assignments, in fact. Learn the difference between formal and informal writing. In this chapter, learn and practice the techniques that can refine your skills.

If your total ranges from 24–37, you consider your writing skills to be average. This is a good start, and you will get a chance to practice your writing skills often in your online education. Even in discussions, you will be required to write. In other assignments, your writing may need to be more formal. In this chapter, you will learn how to hone your writing skills, which will be important in your education and future career success.

If your total ranges from 10–23, you believe you need to build writing skills. The good news is that you will get a lot of practice to do just that while taking online courses. The best way to improve any skill is to practice it. Before you begin, make sure you understand the assignment. Then implement one or two of the strategies in this chapter. When you feel comfortable, implement a couple more. Find any writing opportunity you can, and you will become quite competent and confident.

Analyze: Why are writing skills so important in online courses?

> The ability to write well will be valuable in many situations throughout your online program and your future career.

On average, online courses are very writing intensive. Though you may communicate informally in writing frequently—in e-mail, instant messaging, blogs, or on social networking sites—writing academic papers and assignments requires more thought, concentration, structure, and effort.

English teachers have long known that one of the most important ways to build writing skills is to write more often. As an online student, you will have opportunities to improve this important skill in a variety of assignments.

Regardless of the type of assignment, the most important way to improve your academic writing skills is to strengthen your critical thinking ability. The quality of your writing depends on the quality of the thinking you do. Writing allows you to analyze problems, solutions, ideas, or topics and then expand on what you know. By providing a great way to clearly organize and stimulate your thoughts, writing enhances your active thinking processes.

Most online classes are heavily oriented toward written assignments such as the following:

- Essays
- Research reports
- Case studies
- Application exercises
- Responses to articles
- Discussion forums
- Quizzes and exams
- Presentations

Understanding Assignments

When you write for all types of online course assignments, remember that most of these are graded! This may seem obvious, but there can be a tendency for online students, especially at first, to treat course assignments informally.

Before You Begin

The first step is to understand the assignment. The requirements may be in the form of an outline or a description. They might also be stated as a one-line entry in your syllabus or as a short essay question. If you have questions about what is expected, ask your instructor for clarification. Make sure you know the following aspects of the assignment:

- *Purpose.* The first question you should have of any assignment is "What is the purpose of this assignment?" Assignments are usually written to meet one or more of the learning objectives for the unit. Identify the learning objective that is covered by your assignment.

- *Deadline.* Mark this date on your calendar, along with any milestones, such as creating an outline or writing a first draft, that you need to complete before the project is due.

- *Format of the assignment.* Is there a minimum or a maximum length? Your assignment may specify length as being an approximate number of words (a single-spaced document with line breaks between paragraphs and a one-inch margin is usually about 500 words per page).

- *Method for submission.* For example, you may be asked to send your assignments as attachments to e-mail, in the body of an e-mail message, with FTP (file transfer protocol), as an upload to the Web, or via fax. Also verify the naming convention you should use for your file.

If you need technical directions, such as how to save a document in a particular format or how to upload and download files within the learning management system, make sure you have those directions or ask for them immediately if you do not.

- *Help features.* Help is only a click away in an online course. Online courses often also offer a host of campus services that are accessible from within the site, including academic advising, financial aid information and forms, services for students with disabilities, 24/7 libraries, and online tutoring. You instructor can also be a great resource if you get stuck. Ask for help as soon as you need it.

- *Level of thinking required.* In some online assignments, you might be asked to simply remember facts and recall them or you may be asked to apply what you are learning to new situations. Different levels of thinking are illustrated in Key 7.1. Understanding the level of thinking the instructor is looking for in each writing assignment can help (see Keys 7.2 and 7.3).

- *Grading criteria.* "How will this be graded?" Knowing the answer to this question will help you identify what you need to do within the assignment. The grading criteria might simply be a list of the elements that should be included or it can be a rubric that lists the criteria and assigns points for increasing levels of sophistication. If it is a group assignment, will the group and individual portions be graded? What is the assignment worth to you personally? How much of your grade is it? What skills can you gain from doing it? Your answer determines the level of effort you want to put into it. Not all writing assignments warrant the same level of effort.

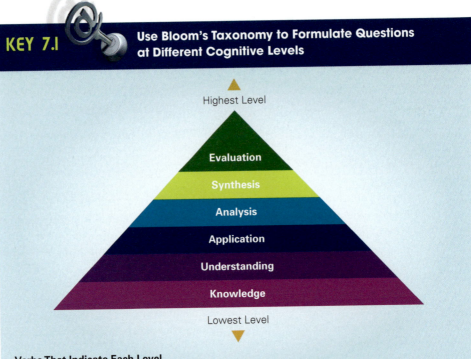

KEY 7.1   Use Bloom's Taxonomy to Formulate Questions at Different Cognitive Levels

Highest Level

Evaluation

Synthesis

Analysis

Application

Understanding

Knowledge

Lowest Level

Verbs That Indicate Each Level

1. **Knowledge:** average, define, duplicate, label, list, memorize, name, order, recognize, relate, recall, repeat, reproduce, state.

2. **Understanding:** classify, describe, discuss, explain, express, identity, indicate, locate, recognize, report, restate, review, select, translate.

3. **Application:** apply, choose, demonstrate, dramatize, employ, illustrate, interpret, operate, practice, schedule, sketch, solve, use, write.

4. **Analysis:** analyze, appraise, calculate, categorize, compare, contrast, criticize, differentiate, discriminate, distinguish, examine, experiment, question, test.

5. **Synthesis:** arrange, assemble, collect, compose, construct, create, design, develop, formulate, manage, organize, plan, prepare, propose, set up, write.

6. **Evaluation:** appraise, argue, assess, attach, choose, compare, defend, estimate, judge, predict, rate, score, select, support, value, evaluate.

Question Types	Examples
General knowledge: Identify and recall information (who, what, when, where, how)	Describe . . .
Comprehension: Organize and select facts and ideas	Retell . . .
Application: Use facts, rules, and principles	How is this an example of . . . ? How is this related to . . . ? Why is this significant?
Analysis: Separate a whole into component parts	What are the parts or features of . . . ? Classify this according to . . . Provide an outline or diagram of . . . How does this compare/contrast with . . . ? What evidence can you list for . . . ?
Synthesis: Combine ideas to form a new whole	What would you predict/infer from . . . ? What ideas can you add to . . . ? How would you create/design a new . . . ? What might happen if you combined . . . ? What solutions would you suggest for . . . ?
Evaluation: Develop opinions, judgments, or decisions	Do you agree . . . ? What do you think about . . . ? What is the most important . . . ? Place the following in order of priority . . . How would you decide about . . . ? What criteria would you use to assess . . . ?

Approaching Different Types of Assignments

Discussion Questions

An instructor's assessment of your knowledge will be substantially based on your contributions to class discussions. Most instructors do not grade or read every post, but from following the discussions, they have a good sense of how well you understand the course material. One of the biggest problems for students in discussions is not taking them seriously at first. Your responses to discussion questions matter to your overall course grade.

In a discussion forum, it is especially important to show respect for each other's ideas. Even within the more adversarial style of a debate, discussions can be hindered and stifled by confrontational tones.

It is difficult to read tone, such as humor and sarcasm, over electronic communication. There is often a disconnect that happens between the time you write something and the time someone reads your post. What you meant to sound funny may actually be interpreted as callous or harsh. Your well-intended polite disagreement with someone may be taken as mean-spirited. It is important to give little cues to help the reader know which tone to add to the words they are reading. When

You may be required to post a comment and respond to others' comments, which may be posted over several days, so be sure to plan this into your week.

Part of critical thinking is the ability to empathetically understand another person's experience. Try to see things from others' points of view.

Online assignments that ask you to:	Require you to:
Define, label, list, name, repeat, order, arrange	Memorize, recall, and present information
Describe, indicate, restate, explain, review, summarize, classify	Interpret information in your own words
Apply, illustrate, prepare, solve, use, sketch, operate, practice, calculate	Apply knowledge to new situations
Analyze, categorize, compare, test, distinguish, examine, contrast	Break down knowledge into parts and show relationships among parts
Arrange, compose, formulate, organize, plan, assemble, construct	Bring together parts of knowledge to form a whole; build relationships for new situations
Appraise, evaluate, conclude, judge, predict, compare, score	Make judgments based on criteria; support, confirm preferences
Use supporting examples, cite passages from the text, paraphrase, summarize	Quote or paraphrase to support what you have written
Provide corroborating evidence, reference other works, research, cite examples from case studies	Use outside research to support your thesis or hypothesis

KEY 7.4   Strategies for Discussion Responses

Address people by name. Begin by referring to the person to whom you are responding. (John, I just finished reading your post and . . .)

Offer a positive comment about the post. (I really appreciated your comments about . . . or That is such an important consideration when dealing with . . .)

Do what you can to convey your meaning. Love them or not, emoticons can be quite helpful in distinguishing your tone. A smiley face after a correction, disagreement, or joke can let the reader know your intentions in writing the comment.

Don't type in all caps. All caps can translate as "shouting" in the online world.

Know your audience. Should you write more formally or less formally? Consider that it's very easy to forward messages. Write carefully.

Refrain from posting while angry or frustrated. Write your message if you need to when angry, but don't post until some time has passed. Read it again and modify it as you think best.

If possible, read others' messages before posting. Often someone may have already begun addressing the points. You may be able to build on these comments.

your tone communicates attack, then you are much less likely to be successful at convincing anyone of your point of view. It is best to avoid negativity and sarcasm.

To help ensure that your comments are received with the professionalism and respect you intended and to accomplish the goals of the assignment, try the strategies in Key 7.4 for responding to discussion posts.

Essays

Common types of essays that are required in online courses assignments include the following:

- *Process essay.* Explanation of how something works or how to do something.

- *Comparison essay.* Examination of similarities and differences between two or more subjects. For example, you might compare one computer to another. In this structure, facts and ideas are presented that show similarities or differences.

- *Cause/effect essay.* Analysis of a subject with clear cause-and-effect connections between the points. You show what has happened and who or what made it happen.

- *Problem/solution essay.* Detailed examination of a subject with a full discussion of possible solutions. You examine problems from different angles before proposing any solutions.

Using the grading rubric in Key 7.5 for a discussion question on leadership, create an initial response to the question given after the following quote and contextual paragraph.

> For scientific leadership, give me Scott; for swift and efficient travel, give me Amundsen; but when you are in a hopeless situation and there appears to be no way out, get down on your knees and pray for Shackleton.
>
> —Raymond Priestly

Consider this quote about Ernest Shackleton, who was the captain of the ship named *Endurance,* which set off on December 7, 1914, carrying the first crew to attempt crossing the Antarctic continent on foot. They never made it. The ship became trapped in the crushing ice, in a place where rescue was impossible. All the crew members survived and credited Shackleton with getting everyone safely through a miraculous, harrowing journey of 22 months across stormy, icy seas.

Refer to the quote as you respond to the following prompt:

Identify what you think are the two most important characteristics of a good leader and explain your reasoning.

- *Response to an article or multimedia presentation.* Reaction to reading an article, watching a video, or engaging in a multimedia interactivity. This might be a logical analysis of the main points and conclusions. It might be an emotional reaction to the author's premise. Whatever the assignment, your thoughts should be well organized and follow a structure. If you can't think of a place to start, consider these questions:
  - What were your feelings after reading the opening paragraph or watching the introduction? The middle? The end?
  - What connections are there between the information presented and your life?
  - Who else should learn the information?

KEY 7.5   Sample Grading Rubric

Initial Posting 25 points maximum	Exemplary (22–25 points)	Acceptable (18–21 points)	Minimal acceptance (0–17 points)
	Initial post is original, thought-provoking, and displays an excellent understanding of the course materials and the underlying concept being discussed. Uses course materials and other information to support important points.	Initial post is acceptable but does not consistently demonstrate higher-order thinking. Displays some understanding of the course materials and the underlying concept being discussed. Limited use of course materials and other information to support points.	Initial post is vague, incomplete, or displays little understanding of the course materials and the underlying concept being discussed. Uses low-level thinking. Course materials and other information to support points is incoherent or missing entirely.
	Initial post is made in a timely manner (allowing adequate time for peers to respond).	Initial post is made late in the timeline of the module (allowing limited time for peers to respond).	Initial post is made so that peers have inadequate time to respond.

- What is the most important point?
- Do you think the title fits?
- Did it help you learn something?
- What questions did it bring up that you would like answered?

- *Persuasive essay.* Justification of a claim about a topic with specific evidence. You will want to make a fair, respectful, and thoughtful consideration of any counterarguments and then determine how to deal with opposing views.

Some additional strategies for improving your essay writing are shown in Key 7.6.

Application Exercises

Exercises are usually problem-solving assignments and are often found in the math and science areas. When faced with application exercises that require you to use learned material, pay careful attention to detail, particularly when following written directions.

When grading these types of exercises, the instructor will look for competence in the work submitted. This means that all of the required steps have been followed and the material is presented in a professional manner.

Group Assignments

Working with students of differing skill and experience levels can be both educational and problematic. The variety among people who study online will probably only increase, however, and group work will be required in many online courses.

Strategies for working on online group writing projects are highlighted in Key 7.7.

Tests and Quizzes

Most exams and quizzes are open book for online courses. In this case, you will be able to use all available resources during the exam. Though open book tests and quizzes may elicit less fear than other tests, it is important not to underestimate the preparation you will need for these exams. Before you take an exam or quiz, spend some time organizing your notes and materials so you can quickly find data, quotes,

KEY 7.6   Strategies for Online Essay Assignments

Learn your word processing program and how to use it. You should know how to use the spell-check, grammar, and language utilities. Know how to copy and paste, format, find and replace, and use other convenient tools. In some programs, you can keep track of your sources and create bibliographies.

Be aware of discipline-specific differences. Every academic discipline has its own language and conventions in terms of tone and style. Review style manuals such as the MLA and APA style guides.

Learn from your mistakes. Are there patterns of strengths and weaknesses in your writing that instructors frequently mention? Consciously work on improving your weaknesses and use your strengths regularly.

Read often. By reading good writing, you will improve your sentence structure, spelling, punctuation, and vocabulary. Analyze examples of good writing, and consider keeping a file of writing samples and notations about what works and what does not.

Write often. Look for writing opportunities. Keep a journal. Volunteer to take minutes of meetings and write summaries of group decisions for your group projects. Focus on specific skills each time you write.

Implement the 10-minute rule if you get stuck. If you get "writer's block," usually caused by anxiety, try focusing for just 10 minutes and force yourself to write freely about anything related to a part of the topic you find interesting.

Manage document versions. Typically, all group members will contribute to the written group assignment. This can lead to chaos if the document version is not controlled. One way to manage version control is to have only one person working on the document at a time. Make sure you know how to insert comments and track changes (refer to the tutorials and help topics in your software) or agree to color-code each member's additions. Most word processing and presentation software also allow you to compare documents and accept or reject changes. Assigning one person as "owner" of the document may help you manage all the changes.

Ensure compatibility of group documents. Prior to any work being done, groups should agree on which software to use and the format for all documents or presentations.

Have a kick-off telephone call if possible with all members. You can use a free conference service to arrange the call, such as freeconference.com. Select a facilitator for the call through e-mail or your discussion area. Then have a clear agenda and purpose. Before you speak, state who you are. The facilitator should summarize the conversation at the end of the meeting.

Title any group papers and presentations. Include the authors and date of creation and submission. Try to make the title of your presentation interesting and thought-provoking.

examples, and arguments to use in answers. Make your reference materials as user-friendly as possible to not lose time looking for information during the test.

Key 7.8 shows strategies for taking an open book exam. Not all online tests are open book or self-monitored. Online schools use a variety of testing methods for different courses:

- *Pop-up chat quiz.* At any time during class time or a test, the instructor can connect to students via the class chat system and do a sort of on-the-spot pop quiz.

- *Simultaneous timed tests.* Tests are scheduled with set time limits so students don't have time to research. Sometimes, even individual questions are timed, for a more controlled test environment.

- *Monitored tests.* Some schools require students to attend a site where assistants monitor as they take the test in person.

Manage your time. Usually, you have a certain window of time to take an exam, and oftentimes, there is a little clock on the screen that can unnerve you if you are unprepared for it. Keep in mind that when you take tests from home, anything can and will happen—your neighbor will suddenly knock on your door to deliver Girl Scout cookies, telemarketers will call, children will wake up, the dog will want to be let out, and so on. Be prepared for distractions.

Predict exam questions. It may be beneficial to keep a running page of predicted test questions. As you read through a chapter, ask yourself many questions at the end of each section. When it is time to study for the test, you may have already predicted many of the questions your professor will ask.

Answer easy questions first. If you stumble over difficult questions for too long, you may not be able to complete the exam.

Print a feedback report. Once you submit the quiz or exam for grading, if you can print out a copy of the feedback report or quiz or take screen shots, do this. These are a great resource to study for the next exam. If you get immediate feedback on the quiz or exam, review the questions and answers.

Write down key facts. Before you even look at the test, write down key information, including formulas, rules, and definitions that you don't want to forget.

Start with the big picture. Spend a few minutes at the start gathering information about the questions—how many in each section, what types, and their point values. Use this information to schedule your time.

Directions count, so read them. Reading test directions carefully can save you trouble. For example, you may be required to answer only one of three essay questions or you may be informed of penalties given for incorrect responses to short-answer questions.

Mark up the questions. Mark up instructions and key words to avoid careless errors. Circle qualifiers—words and phrases that can alter a sentence's meaning—such as *always, never, all, none, sometimes,* and *every;* verbs that communicate specific

instructions; and concepts that are tricky or need special attention.

Be precise when taking a machine-scored test. Use the right pencil (usually a no. 2) on machine-scored tests, and mark your answer in the correct space, filling it completely. (Use a straight edge to focus on the correct line for each question.) Periodically, check the answer number against the question number to make sure they match.

Work from easy to hard. Begin with the easiest questions and answer them quickly without sacrificing accuracy. This will boost your confidence and leave more time for harder questions.

Watch the clock. If you are worried about time, you may rush through the test and have time left over. When this happens, check over your work instead of leaving early. If, on the other hand, you are falling behind, be flexible about the best use of your remaining time.

Ask for clarification. Sometimes a simple re-wording will make you realize that you really know the material.

Skip the question and come back to it later. Letting your subconscious mind work on the question sometimes makes a difference.

Build logical connections. Take a calculated risk by using what you already know about the topic.

Create a visual picture. Make a mental map. Remembering where material was covered in your notes and text may jog your memory about content as well.

Just start writing. The act of writing about related material may help you recall the targeted information. You may want to do this kind of "freewriting" on a spare scrap of paper, think about what you've written, and then write your final answer on the test paper or booklet.

Show what you *do* know. While most instructors will deduct points for this approach, they may also give partial credit because you showed that you know the material.

There are general strategies for real-time, monitored tests that will also help you handle almost any test, including short-answer and essay exams.

Key 7.9 contains advice for taking real-time exams.

Take a strategic approach to questions you cannot answer Even if you are well prepared, you may face questions you do not understand or cannot answer. Key 7.10 has ideas to consider.

ANSWER the Question

Use the acronym ANSWER to help remember general strategies you can use to approach almost any writing assignment or exercise.

• *Address each part of the question.* Many online assignments have multiple parts, and it is easy to miss one if you aren't careful.

• *Narrow down topics.* If the questions you are asked are not very specific, you will have to determine what to write about. Often this nonspecificity is purposeful. In these cases, part of what you're being judged on is whether you can identify main topics.

• *State definitions of key terms.* When answering a question, you will want to define the important terms (even if already defined in the lesson).

- _**W**rite a topic sentence._ A topic sentence summarizes what you intend to write about in your answer.

- _**E**xplain with examples._ After each topic sentence, provide some kind of explanation or offer examples or other forms of evidence. It is almost never enough to just provide a single-sentence answer.

- _**R**eorganize ideas into logical sequence._ If you have more than one paragraph in your answer, each paragraph should have its own topic sentence and be about something in particular. Organize your paragraphs, or topics, into a logical sequence so that one idea leads into the next.

Characteristics of
Effective Writing

Most college writing consists of assignments that are tailored to help you think about the subject and demonstrate what you have learned. The most effective assignments, essays, and reports include the following characteristics:

- Clear topic
- Good organization with straightforward beginning, middle, and end
- Original material in the writer's own voice
- Variety of sentence types
- Concise
- Grammatically correct
- Well designed to enhance the content

Clear Topic

In writing assignments, you are sometimes given a topic, but often you must find the topic or question that is relevant and appropriate. To choose a topic that helps your readers learn about or understand a subject in a new way, try brainstorming ideas with the following questions:

- What happened? How? When? Why?
- How can the subject be defined?
- Are there exceptions to the rule?
- Are there examples?
- What is the subject similar to or different from?
- What caused this? Why does it occur?
- Are there advantages or disadvantages to discuss?
- Are any current events related to the topic?

Next, do some exploratory research beyond your course materials about the subject. As you review the literature or read in a particular area, you may note ideas that will help you get started with the writing.

Good Organization

Good written submissions are logically organized with a distinct beginning, middle, and ending. The opening is interesting and states the purpose of the writing. The middle supports each point with examples, explanations, definitions, and details.

CREATE

Create a New Topic

Think of any subject you're interested in. Next, brainstorm. From what you know of this subject already, fill in the following blanks:

1. This topic reminds me of _____.
2. I'm not sure whether this can also mean _____.
3. In regard to this topic I'm surprised that _____.
4. Because of _____, it means that _____.
5. I wonder if _____.
6. When _____ happens, then _____.
7. Before _____.
8. I am sure that _____.
9. Maybe if _____, then _____.

What new topics came to mind?

The ending ties up or clarifies certain points. It helps the reader see the purpose and importance of your message.

You may also organize a paper by stating a problem, exploring possible solutions, and concluding with what you've decided is the best solution, along with detailed reasons why. Or you can order information chronologically or spatially or in another format suitable for argument or analysis that you develop depending on the content.

Writer's Own Material and Voice

Everyone has a different way of writing. You can speak through your writing in a sincere, natural way, using a bit of creativity, even in academic writing. Resist the urge to impress by using inflated language or page counts, but do keep your audience and purpose in mind. Your goal in most academic writing is to convey facts about a subject, integrate opinions based on facts, and synthesize what you have learned as you go along.

Similar to choosing between dressing up in formal clothes or wearing jeans, different words have different effects for different occasions. Your tone of writing, like the way you dress, determines how your audience will perceive you and your topic.

Plagiarism

Many students are under the impression one only needs to cite material when using a direct quote. However, anytime you take an idea, thought, or theory from another author or text, a citation must be used.

When you get excited about writing something, it can be easy to overlook the obvious: You must give credit to the resources for your material. Not doing so is plagiarism, which is a very serious academic offense, sometimes resulting in expulsion from school.

It is increasingly easy to forget to cite sources with advancing technology and abundant information available for the easy cut-and-paste feature of most text readers and word processing programs.

Scenario: You are reading from a website and see a great quote you'd like to use. You quickly cut and paste it into your notes. Then . . . the tea kettle starts whistling, the dog starts

JANE

**Online student
Age 35**

CHALLENGE

Writing Papers

Though this is somewhat time-consuming, I live by my strategy of writing papers! Because any paper I write usually needs research, I do the following:

As I go through the research, I often find quotes or significant points that are key to my topic.

I type in each of these quotes or points, along with the page number and resource. Once I've gotten to where I feel that I have enough research, I go back through my document of quotes and points. For each and every one of these, I write a one-line summary (or less) that I bold. I then take those bolded summaries and move just those into a new document. Within that document, I create an outline with subheadings. When I have an outline I'm happy with, I go back to my original document and retrieve all the quotes and informational points and move them into place under the appropriate summary. Then everything is in order.

From there, I can start writing around the quotes and points. I do this by first taking every single one and writing an introduction to it in my own words. I relate it contextually to the rest of the information I have chosen. Then I summarize and connect it to the main point. After that, I continue to refine by researching and finding additional points and creating new connections.

barking . . . you get up to get your tea and see to the dog . . . Returning to the computer, you may forget to note the author. Innocent enough, but you've just risked committing plagiarism later on, when you incorporate the knowledge you obtained but forget to cite the site! Many instructors have access to plagiarism software that can quickly determine if your submission is too similar to information on the Internet or other reference sources.

Sentence Variety

Sentences vary in length and begin in many ways. Mixing up words and phrases to build sentences that sound different can give your writing life and rhythm. Too many sentences with the same structure and length can grow monotonous for readers. Long sentences work well for incorporating a lot of information, and short sentences help maximize crucial points. Too many sentences starting with the same word can grow tedious for readers.

Conciseness

Concise writing does not always have the fewest words but always uses the strongest. Adjectives appear somewhat sparingly. Nouns and verbs are specific. Some sentences can easily be combined, and you may be able to get rid of vague words. Use a thesaurus to help find the best word.

Correct Grammar and Punctuation

Grammatical mistakes, typos, and disorganization can lead the reader to assume that you are sloppy and careless. Fortunately, spell-check and grammar utilities are found on almost all word processing and e-mail programs, allowing you to check and correct your errors.

Proofreading

Proofreading allows you to check for errors in grammar, punctuation, spelling, capitalization, and proper word usage. Proofread all assignments. Though your word processing program can probably detect grammar and spelling errors, they don't catch everything.

Wordy: Some observers have noted that when a larger rock is in motion, such as when it is rolling down a hill or incline, it is not as likely to be covered with the green growth that stationary, unmoving objects tend to exhibit. (41 words)

Concise: A rolling stone gathers no moss. (6 words)

Avoid misusing pronouns. Overuse of the personal pronoun can make your work seem overly subjective. Gendered pronouns can cause readers to feel excluded. If you use *he* and *him* all the time, you may be alienating half your potential readership. Instead, alternate genders and use plurals when possible.

You can also review your paper for grammatical errors:

- Do subjects and verbs agree?
- Are pronouns clear and in agreement?
- Are there any sentence fragments, comma splices, or run-on sentences?
- Are list items and sentences parallel?
- Are verb tenses consistent?
- Are there clear transitions between ideas and paragraphs?

Getting Feedback

Feedback is especially important in an online course, in which you don't have face-to-face interaction. After you've gone through the document as carefully as possible, ask a reliable classmate or friend to do the same. Not all peer feedback is equal, however. When you solicit feedback, evaluate it for relevance to your revision. For especially valuable feedback, give your classmates a checklist of items for particular attention.

Peer Reviews for Written Assignments

Many online group assignments require you to read classmates' papers and give constructive feedback on topics such as the following:

- *Purpose.* Is this clear?
- *Audience.* Who is the audience? Is the tone appropriate for them? Will they understand the message? Is it written at the appropriate level given the audience's knowledge of the topic?
- *Ideas.* Are concepts well developed? Are the key terms defined?
- *Organization.* Is the paper organized in a logical manner? Does it flow from topic to topic?

Common Mistakes Found in Papers

Affect vs. Effect

Affect means "to influence" or "to act in a way that you don't feel," whereas *effect* refers to a result.

You can be affected by an effect.

Example: The amount of snow affects the mountain conditions, leading to road closures and other hazardous effects.

Who vs. Whom

Use *who* when it's the subject and *whom* when it's the object of the sentence.

Example: Who kissed whom?

Which vs. That

Which is for use in sentences that have extra, non-essential information added. You can remove this piece of a sentence without losing the essential meaning.
That is for immediately important information. You can't remove what follows without losing meaning.

Example: The letter that changed everything arrived from Germany.

The letter, which was from Germany, informed me that I won the lottery.

Me vs. I

In order to determine whether you are using the right form, take out any reference to other people and see whether the sentence makes sense.

Example: John and I went to the concert. "Me went to the concert" doesn't sound right.

Its vs. It's

Usually, the possessive of any word ends in an apostrophe plus *s,* so we want to use *it's* to mean "belonging to it." However, in this case, *it's* is a contraction for "it is."

Weather vs. Whether

Weather refers to the climate. *Whether* is a conjunction that introduces possibilities or alternatives.

Example: We are going skiing tomorrow whether the weather cooperates or it doesn't.

There, Their, and They're

There refers to a place. *Their* indicates possession. *They're* is a contraction of the words *they* and *are.*
Example: They're going over there to get their belongings.

- *Readability.* How enjoyable and easy-to-read was the essay? Did you have to struggle to extract the meaning?

Be very specific in your feedback. Saying "Great job" does not help the writer. Focus on something like "The personal story in the opening really caught my attention because . . ."

IM 2Day 4 Writing

The lingo and abbreviations used for instant messaging (IM) is evidence of the evolution of language and may someday be a legitimate form that will be taught in English class. However, that day has not yet arrived.

This shorthand can be quite helpful to communicate or spark thinking and is fine to use if it helps in the early stages of writing; just be sure to avoid it in your submitted assignment. The same way you employ a different language structure while watching a heated football game than you do at work, you should reserve IM language for appropriate situations.

Good Design

Bad design can ruin all your good words. Although some academic writing must follow strict guidelines in terms of layout and design, other assignments will be up to your discretion. For these, note that some online instructors print out assignments, read and make comments on the hard copy, and then send their notes to the student by e-mail. Other instructors, wanting to save the time, read and mark the papers onscreen. You will want to design your assignments for both types of readers.

Key 7.11 details several techniques to ensure your essay's meaning is clear and the writing is easy to read.

KEY 7.11   Design Considerations for Online Assignments

Be careful when copying information from a text editor into your e-mail program. The formatting capabilities of e-mail messages are not the same as text editors, such as Microsoft Word, and your formatting can be altered. Learn how to attach your assignments to your submission messages and only use the body of the e-mail message for actual content when explicitly told to do so.

Supply titles, subtitles, and bold subheadings. Hierarchical divisions help the reader skim the paper. If you don't put the subheadings in when you first write the assignment, you can add them afterward. Be careful when using clever titles—they may liven up a document but can also get in the way of understanding.

Use short paragraphs and borders. Short paragraphs with a topic sentence and only one main thought in each can help the reader quickly find needed information.

Pay attention to line spacing and font sizes. Make sure that lines are not too close together and the font is not too small. Your instructor may have spe-

cific guidelines. If not, essays should be 10-point to 12-point type, with 1-inch margins, double-spaced, and preferably in Times New Roman font. Avoid unique fonts that look interesting but are not formal (i.e., Comic Sans).

Be consistent with terms. Format URL addresses consistently, for instance.

Use emphasis sparingly. Especially for academic writing, italics and underlining are the preferred way to emphasize words or phrases when necessary. The use of all caps and emoticons is not recommended for formal papers and assignments. Bold is usually for headings, subheadings, and titles. Choose one method to use consistently throughout an essay, but be careful not to overuse effects. Instead, try to express any emphasis primarily through your words themselves.

Test your e-mail messages. If you are submitting an assignment via e-mail or as an attachment, test it by sending it to yourself. Always double-check your sent mail to ensure that attachments were indeed attached.

Intelligence		Strategies
Verbal-Linguistic		As you revise your document, digitally record and play back both the old and new versions. Speaking and hearing them read aloud immediately after writing can help you to "step back" and analyze your work.
		Use a screen reader program as you read to both read and hear the paper. At the same time you are listening, you can also write comments and evaluations in a second window.
		When doing a peer review, make comments into a digital voice recorder, then transfer that recording into the computer and forward it as an attachment.
Logical-Mathematical		Organize information into ideas and manipulate the ideas as blocks of text to create outlines.
Bodily-Kinesthetic		Use note cards to arrange notes in different orders and sequences around the room. Develop an outline that can start your writing.
		Write while you are standing at your computer.
Visual-Spatial		Use a visual map to discover new ideas in a visual way. Begin by putting your topic idea in the center and drawing radiating lines out from it. At the end of each of these lines, or rays, write down all the ideas that occur to you. Brainstorm for a period of time, such as two minutes, and generate several different ideas.
		Combine maps from different subjects to brainstorm topic ideas.
		Manipulate digital text by copying and pasting and then changing it to modify its meaning. Find key elements in the text and create new meaning by replacing these elements with alternatives.
		Use a Venn Diagram (overlapping circles) to compare and contrast different ideas.
Interpersonal		Collaborate with others, sharing the writing experience. If your course does not offer this opportunity, search for learning communities or use social networking sites to find students studying the same topic.
		Talk to as many people as you can about your topic and get feedback during all phases of the writing process.
Intrapersonal		Much of the writing process is a naturally intrapersonal experience. If this is your learning style preference, you are in luck! Your challenge will be to step outside yourself to see how others view your writing. Imagine that you are teaching someone else the material. Does it flow logically?
Musical		Find the rhythm in the writing of others you admire. Notice how the sentence structure varies and the style flows. Try to apply that sense of rhythm to your writing. Try with other rhythms you notice.
Naturalistic		Bring a laptop or notebook outside to a place that inspires you and write there.
		As you outline your writing, consider other items that might fit into the same category as your subject.

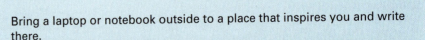

Collaborative Writing

Online courses sometimes offer the opportunity for collaborative writing—informal discussion and shared writing with others in a dedicated space. Students collaborate and get feedback from many other writers. It can be quite helpful to increase motivation and energy about a topic. In collaborative writing, students help each other generate ideas and peer edit each other's papers. Rather than receiving a series of separate, individual reviews, writers can build on the comments of others online. Collaborative writing environments allow students to interact with peers at every stage of the writing process.

There are numerous ways to write collaboratively, including the following:

- Blogs
- Wikis
- Learning management system chat room and document sharing features.

- Microblogs, such as Twitter.com
- Web conferencing software
- Discussion forums

Applying Strategies
for Different Learning Styles

Use your strengths to help you improve your test-taking skills. Can you apply any of the additional suggestions in Key 7.12 here?

Though students wonder about much of the information they learn in school and how they will ever use it again, writing is a skill people use every day. Throughout your life, you will frequently communicate informally—and occasionally, formally. Knowing how to effectively get your points across in writing can have a big impact on your future success.

PRACTICE & plan apply

Thesis: College students should be required to participate in a community service project before graduation in order to increase their maturity and community awareness.

PLAN

If you were asked to expand on this statement, give examples of your responses to the following assignments:

- Discuss
- Illustrate
- Contrast
- Critique
- Justify, prove, or argue

APPLY

Choose one of the formats and develop a written answer of three to four paragraphs.

CREATING
e-Portfolios

8

DEVELOPING YOUR E-PORTFOLIO

- Purposes of e-Portfolios
- What to Include

STEPS IN CREATING AN E-PORTFOLIO

- Decide
- Collect
- Develop
- Evaluate
- Share

ASK YOURSELF

Do you have a system for keeping track of your accomplishments and the skills you are gaining in school?

IN THIS CHAPTER

you'll explore answers to the following questions:

- What is an e-portfolio?
- Why is an e-portfolio useful?
- What is typically included in an e-portfolio?
- How can you develop an e-portfolio?

Analyze

Taking a self-assessment can help you think more deeply about your own skills and preferences. Consider the questions in this assessment and your responses. What information does this quiz provide about yourself that you can use to develop or improve important skills?

Rate Yourself as a Self-Promoter

For each statement, circle the number that feels right to you, from 1 for "not true for me" to 5 for "very true for me."

▶ I keep track of my accomplishments.   1 2 3 4 5

▶ I often keep samples of my work.   1 2 3 4 5

▶ I am engaged in self-promotion.   1 2 3 4 5

▶ I am familiar with different e-portfolio development platforms.   1 2 3 4 5

▶ I have a quick summary about myself that is effective.   1 2 3 4 5

▶ I am happy with my current resumé.   1 2 3 4 5

▶ I keep track of the skills that I gain from nonacademic activities and realize they are   1 2 3 4 5
important to my future career success.

▶ I am comfortable managing electronic files.   1 2 3 4 5

▶ I see the advantage in having a portfolio that potential employers can access.   1 2 3 4 5

▶ I understand how my courses and assignments relate to the overall goals of my   1 2 3 4 5
program.

Now total your scores. _____

If your total ranges from 38–50, you consider that you have the skills and willingness to create an e-portfolio. This section can help give you the tools to begin, and your creativity and decisions will drive the end product.

If your total ranges from 24–37, you consider that you need some preparation before you're ready to create an e-portfolio. In this chapter, you will learn about the common elements in an e-portfolio and begin creating what you need to populate yours.

If your total ranges from 10–23, you believe you need new skills and more understand about creating an e-portfolio. Because e-portfolios are becoming a popular means to showcase talents and accomplishments, in this section you will learn how they are used and what you can do to begin to develop yours.

Analyze: Why is an e-portfolio important in your education and for your future career?

> Creating an e-portfolio is valuable for two reasons: It helps you reflect on your learning and why each course is important, and it showcases your knowledge and skills to others (i.e., employers).

Going to school, writing papers, doing projects, working full or part time, participating in activities—you are doing and learning a lot. How can you showcase your learning, skills, and achievements?

An electronic portfolio, also known as an *e-portfolio,* is a collection of work that shows evidence of your capabilities, put together and managed by you. It is usually hosted on the Web to allow easy access for selected viewers. E-portfolios are similar to traditional portfolios in providing a space to collect your accomplishments and reflect on your learning and experiences (though some studies have shown that they lead to even better learning outcomes than do paper-based portfolios).*

E-portfolios are becoming more and more popular. Many colleges now require them as a capstone project before graduation to help measure whether students have met the learning outcomes essential to their career and personal success. Have you ever wondered why you are taking general education courses, for instance? Colleges that require an e-portfolio can help you make sense of your learning experiences by asking you to reflect on what you have done and how it relates to the objectives of your program.

In addition, e-portfolios also allow you to "show off" to the rest of the world— whether to a local scholarship committee or a potential employer. They help you tell the story of your life, list your accomplishments, develop goals, and connect with other people to achieve a career that really matters to you. They represent your individual identity and are often an ongoing process of creation.

Developing Your e-Portfolio

An e-portfolio can be seen as a type of learning record that provides actual evidence of achievement.

Purposes of e-Portfolios

E-portfolios are primarily used for the following:

- Storing documents
- Reflecting on learning
- Showcasing achievements for accountability or employment
- Creating a plan of study
- Maintaining a dynamic resumé of your experiences and knowledge

---

*Van Wesel, M., & Prop, A. (2008). *The Influence of Portfolio Media on Student Perceptions and Learning Outcomes.* Retrieved April 10, 2010, from www.fdewb.unimaas.nl/EDUC/MASTER/Documents/Proceedings_ S_ICT2008_Final.pdfpage=73

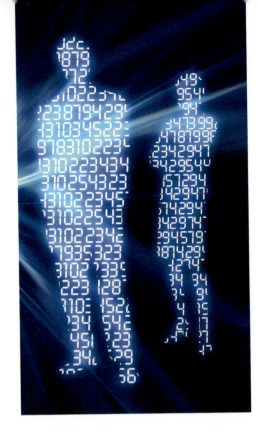

An e-portfolio may include any number of items, including demonstrations—or simply a list—of accomplishments. You can manage and organize different types of material (documents, photos, spreadsheets, etc.) and reflect on the work to demonstrate your self-awareness and understanding.

Your e-portfolio may be solely text-based or it may be graphically enhanced with multimedia elements that might include audio, video, images, blog entries, or hyperlinks to other web pages. By customizing your e-portfolio, you can create a unique, personal, thoughtful, and professional presentation of who you are while demonstrating your abilities and skills.

Depending on the platform you use to create and host your e-portfolio, you can also control who can see your work. Some e-portfolio applications permit varying degrees of audience access, so the same portfolio might be used for multiple purposes.

More than just a catalog, your e-portfolio should be a living document that allows you to reflect on your developing abilities and understandings over time. They can easily be maintained and updated, allowing you to add and modify based on your latest achievements and learning while showing your journey through the learning process.

What to Include

If your school requires an e-portfolio, you will likely be given a list of sections to include and specific instructions on the items within each section. If you have flexibility, you will have to choose the design and structure of your e-portfolio.

Common sections within e-portfolios include the following:

- Welcome Page
- About Me
- Resumé
- Courses
  - Learning Outcomes
  - Sample Coursework
  - Reflection
- Goals
- Community Service and Nonacademic Activities
- Links
- Seminars and Certifications
- Contact Information
- References

Welcome Page

Welcome people to your e-portfolio (see Key 8.1) and tell them about its contents—samples and descriptions of your coursework at college, statements of goals, a listing of your extracurricular activities, and a resumé. You should also tell them how to navigate your e-portfolio.

About Me

Introduce yourself more fully but only reveal details that you would feel comfortable letting most people know (see Key 8.2).

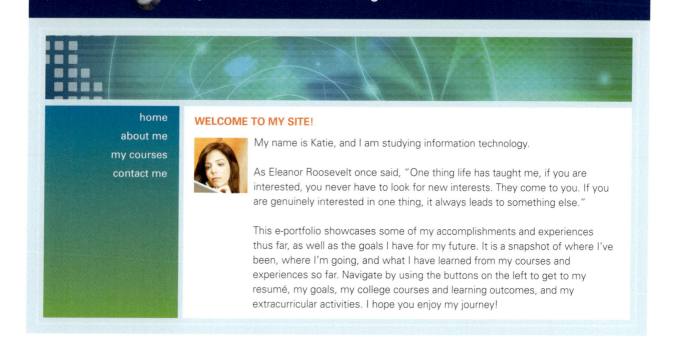

WELCOME TO MY SITE!

My name is Katie, and I am studying information technology.

As Eleanor Roosevelt once said, "One thing life has taught me, if you are interested, you never have to look for new interests. They come to you. If you are genuinely interested in one thing, it always leads to something else."

This e-portfolio showcases some of my accomplishments and experiences thus far, as well as the goals I have for my future. It is a snapshot of where I've been, where I'm going, and what I have learned from my courses and experiences so far. Navigate by using the buttons on the left to get to my resumé, my goals, my college courses and learning outcomes, and my extracurricular activities. I hope you enjoy my journey!

home
about me
my courses
contact me

Give a short biography on this page, listing your background, interests, and other information of your choosing. What do you want to get out of your college experience? What skills or knowledge do you want to acquire? How do you want to grow as a person? As a learner? What kind of career are you looking for? What are your important character traits?

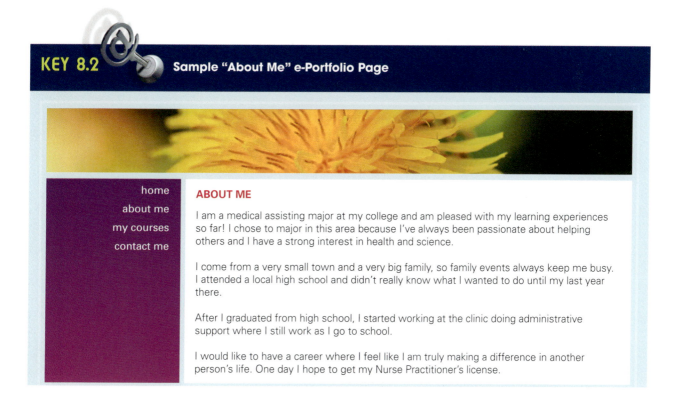

home
about me
my courses
contact me

ABOUT ME

I am a medical assisting major at my college and am pleased with my learning experiences so far! I chose to major in this area because I've always been passionate about helping others and I have a strong interest in health and science.

I come from a very small town and a very big family, so family events always keep me busy. I attended a local high school and didn't really know what I wanted to do until my last year there.

After I graduated from high school, I started working at the clinic doing administrative support where I still work as I go to school.

I would like to have a career where I feel like I am truly making a difference in another person's life. One day I hope to get my Nurse Practitioner's license.

CREATE

Create a Biography

Create your own short biography now by including a little background, one or two of your goals, and something interesting about yourself.

You may include a mission statement on this page, if you choose, and a photograph of yourself, or if you're concerned about privacy, a photo you've taken. Depending on your preferences and resources, you could also include a very short video or slideshow montage of information about yourself.

Resumé

When used in conjunction with your portfolio, your resumé can be a summary as well as an interactive feature (see Key 8.3). You can link to your college's or company's website, to more information about a certification, or even to an audio narration sample of your skills in a second language.

Courses

Keeping track of the courses you take and how they fulfill learning outcomes can give you (and your instructors and potential employers) a sense of how everything is connected.

For each course, you will want to archive one important "signature assignment" and reflect on how your performance on that assignment indicates that you've met the learning outcomes. If your college requires an e-portfolio, your instructors may identify one assignment to include. Other times, you will have to choose from several assignments, so choose the one that best illustrates your effort and learning (see Key 8.4).

Reflective writing allows you to place the assignment in an academic or personal context. How much you write is up to you (or an instructor) but generally, a couple of paragraphs are considered standard.

To get started on reflecting, consider the following questions:

- How does your performance on this assignment demonstrate achievement of—or progress toward—collegewide learning outcomes?
- How does this assignment connect with what you learned in another course?
- What impact did the assignment have on you or your understanding of the world? Did it challenge any of your assumptions?
- What process did you go through to complete the assignment?
- What challenges did you face in completing the assignment?
- How did you address challenges?
- Why did you pick this assignment to put in your e-portfolio?
- What does it demonstrate about your learning?
- How did it help you better understand how the main concepts in this course apply to your life or community?

Bruce K. Manin

2832 Lexington Lane
Denver CO 81503
Phone 555-248-9297
E-mail me@yahoo.com

SUMMARY

Network technician with seven years experience in the military working in a teamwork environment and holding supervisory positions.

EMPLOYMENT HISTORY

YOUR WIRELESS COMPANY

Network Technician—August 2005 to present

* Promoted from Switch Technician, Lucent 5ESS VCDX 2000 switch.
* Serviced and maintained all aspects of the LAN and WAN.
* Inventory control for all office equipment.
* Purchasing configuring and maintaining all computer equipment.
* Roaming billing coordinator.

GENERAL PRODUCTION DEVICES

Electro-Mechanical Assembler—November 2003 to July 2004

* Assembled I.C. (integrated circuit) board component placement machines.
* Made wiring harnesses for these machines.
* Assembled I.O. (input output) boards for these machines.
* Utilized several hand tools and a variety of electronic tools.
* Read blueprints to assemble these machines with various electronic, robotics, pneumatic, and fiber optic components.

COMPUTER SKILLS

Three years of experience with administering LAN and WAN networks. I have approximately twelve years personal computer experience. I am familiar and have worked with Terminal Services, MS-DOS, Windows XP and Vista, and other Microsoft office products. I have installed and configured routers, hubs, network cards, printers, hard drives, CD-ROM drives, zip drives, mother boards, modems, memory and misc. peripherals.

EDUCATION AND TRAINING

My Online College

In process of attaining Bachelor's of Science in Networking

WestSlope IT, Inc., Core Technologies Track. NACSE Associate Network Specialist Certificate.

LANGUAGES

English and German

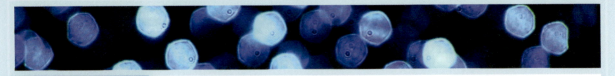

home
about me
my courses
contact me

COURSE NAME: MAT 1001—INTRODUCTION TO STATISTICS

Learning Outcome: Demonstrate mathematical literacy through solving problems, communicating concepts, reasoning mathematically and applying mathematical or statistical methods using multiple representations

Description: In this class we were asked to solve a problem using statistical methods. I met this competency because in this assignment the goal was to recommend an energy solution with fewer environmental and financial consequences. By statistically analyzing data on solar panels, wind turbines, rain collection, and radiation from the night sky, I was able to recommend an alternative energy design solution.

Sample Work: *Windturbine.doc*

Reflection: In writing this paper, I learned quite a bit more about how statistics can be used to see connections and tell a story that is not readily known without the analysis.

My initial thought was that solar energy would be best, but when I analyzed it in terms of several factors, including energy output and cost, my conclusion was that wind turbines were more cost-effective. My data sample only included 30 businesses using each, though. Though statistically significant, there are other issues that may not have been accounted for, including location. Next time I do this type of analysis, I think I'll spend more time thinking the entire problem through before I get my data.

Goals

Include your educational and professional goals. Remember that you can update goals as you progress through your coursework at any time. You can divide them into short-term and long-term goals, if you choose, and reflect on the fit between your personal goals and your program.

Community Service and Nonacademic Activities

External activities can give you many skills and additional knowledge important to your learning and future career. Consider your involvement in the following:

- Clubs
- Intramural sports
- Varsity sports
- Organization memberships
- Leadership
- Media
- Travel
- Service learning
- Internships
- Cooperative learning
- Academic honors
- Tutoring
- Church

- Volunteer work
- International travel
- Other outside activity

Reflect on how your activities have helped you grow as a learner and person.

Other Sections

Include any annotated websites you want visitors to see and your contact information so people can get in touch with you. You may wish to note your blog site, if any, or links to organizations you admire, reflecting on why. Depending on your area of study and expertise, you may include others sections as well. For instance, students in medical fields might create a section titled Clinical Experience whereas business students might prefer a Leadership segment.

Steps in Creating
an e-Portfolio

Before you begin to develop your e-portfolio, explore how other students have created theirs. Once you get a sense of what an e-portfolio can look like and the kind of information they usually provide, you are ready to begin.

The e-portfolio development process usually covers the following stages: Decide, Collect, Develop, Evaluate, Share.

Decide

In this stage, the focus is on the audience for the portfolio and the learning goals that the portfolio should be demonstrating. You will want to make some decisions about what content to have on your site and get a general sense of any features you want to include. How can you use class assignments, such as papers and presentations, to show what you are learning? Do you want to use images? Sound? Video?

Many e-portfolio sites have templates into which you can plug your information. Spend some time exploring the templates and choose one that is clean, easy to navigate, and has a design and style you like.

You do not need a specific kind of computer or special software to make an e-portfolio. The latest versions of web browsers will allow you to create a site and upload files.

Collect

The next step in an e-portfolio is collecting your work. You can use material from multiple applications (word processing, spreadsheets, slideshow creator, video editor, etc.) Create an electronic folder of materials from which you can later select samples of your coursework to put in your e-portfolio. Many e-portfolio platforms allow you to keep personal files, but there may not be enough space for everything. Store everything on your personal computer until you decide definitively what is going in.

Develop

Create your e-portfolio website. If your college requires an e-portfolio, they may offer tutorials or a support service for selected platforms.

Search for at least three samples of online portfolios that other students have created. Scroll through the samples. Which is most effective? Why? Which is least effective? Why?

Otherwise, there are many free options available to create and maintain an e-portfolio, which is basically just a hosted website or blog.

Wordpress: www.wordpress.com

Edublogs: www.edublogs.com

Jimdo.com: www.jimdo.com

Weebly: www.weebly.com

Yola: www.yola.com

You can also use the Google applications GoogleDocs and GoogleSites. Mac users have iWeb to create sites for hosting with a MobileMe account or any other hosting service from an Internet service provider (ISP). If you do have an ISP, you can also create your site in Dreamweaver or similar website.

Platform Considerations

Many options are available, so you may want to consider certain features before deciding which platform to use for your e-portfolio:

• *Ease of use.* Some platforms, including those highlighted in this chapter, use simple drag and drop operations to let you add headings, text blocks, assignment files, photos, audio, and video. Experiment with several to find the one that seems most intuitive for you to use.

• *Storage size.* Most sites offer a sufficient amount of storage space. Consider that a 150-page Microsoft Word document is about 1 MB. Video and photos take up much more space. Large projects and photo galleries are probably best housed at other locations and linked to from within the e-portfolio.

• *Widgets.* Platforms that offer widgets for programs such as Flickr, YouTube, and so on, allow you to store larger media files outside the e-portfolio platform. You can link to these files without taking up storage space or worrying about file upload limits.

• *File-size upload limitations.* Often, file upload limitations are much less than the storage allowed. Though sufficient for many needs, large files of over 5 MB may not be uploaded properly. Check the platform limitations against your design goals before deciding which platform to use.

• *Templates.* Most platforms offer a generous variety of templates to choose among. Peruse the templates of the platforms you are considering.

• *Advertisements.* Make sure the platform you use has a policy of not including advertisements on your pages.

• *Blogs.* Some e-portfolio platforms are blogs whereas others are websites. If you choose a website but want to also include a blog page, make sure your platform allows this.

• *Web-based vs. non-web-based.* A web-based portfolio has a web address (URL) that you can provide to allow others to access it from anywhere. Also, web-based e-portfolios can be accessed and edited from any computer with an up-to-date browser and a good Internet connection.

If your school uses a virtual learning environment (VLE) for the creation of e-portfolios, make sure it can be easily accessed outside the VLE. If not, consider creating a secondary e-portfolio that you can use beyond your school years.

Creating Pages and Uploading Material

Once you decide on the platform to use, you can begin creating your e-portfolio. Building an e-portfolio takes time, so plan for this. Begin by determining the structure of the site. Create the main pages that you decided to include.

Next put in your signature assignments and reflections. If required, make sure your instructor knows these have been included. Organize the materials into a sequence (or with hypermedia links) for the best presentation of the material.

Evaluate

You should evaluate the e-portfolio's effectiveness in light of its purpose and presentation. Similar to proofreading, the evaluation process is when you want to solicit feedback from your instructors and peers.

At this stage, if your platform allows, you can create special guest accounts with user names and passwords so that the evaluators are the only people who can view your site.

Share

Once an e-portfolio is complete, it needs an audience. Just as with any website, the development is only half of the process. Next, you need to get it in front of the people who need to see it. You might need to let your instructors know they can look at it or give the web address to potential employers.

Other tips for developing an e-Portfolio can be found in Key 8.5.

KEY 8.5   **Tips When Building an e-Portfolio**

Back up your work. It does not happen often, but sometimes e-portfolio platforms can lose your data. Keep a digital copy of the work you put in your e-portfolio.

Include only personal information you want to publicly share. An e-portfolio is a public representation of your learning, but you certainly don't have to put your photo, full name, or even contact information if you don't want to. You'll have to decide how best to balance your privacy concerns with the desire to use the tool to showcase your accomplishments.

Password protect only if necessary. Consider your site public if at all possible. Note that even without a password, it will be difficult for someone to find unless you use the platform tools to optimize your site for search engines. Most people will not be able to find your site unless you give them the URL.

Don't pay unless you really want the extra features. You can build an excellent e-portfolio using the free platforms without upgrading to any "pro" features that cost money. The decision whether to upgrade your account to add pro features is entirely up to you.

Know your audience. Use a respectful tone and choose photos appropriate for your audience. If you question the appropriateness of an inclusion, it is better to err on the side of caution and delete it.

ONLINE OUTLOOK

KATIE

Online student
Age 22

CHALLENGE

Understanding
learning objectives

I was required to begin an e-portfolio for my college. For every course we take from here on, we have to have one assignment that illustrates what we did and how that met the course goals. I was very confused at first. I never paid much attention to any learning objectives. I skipped right over them, in fact.

Now, though, I can see the connections. There really is a method to the madness.

I look at the objectives for every class and am always thinking about what I can include in my portfolio.

A big challenge for me was learning the e-portfolio system. We had the choice of using WordPress or Yola, and I chose Yola, but it took me a week to learn how to use it.

PRACTICE & plan apply

Now that you know a little about creating an e-portfolio and what can go in one, it is time to start developing yours.

PLAN

Identify the elements or pages you will include. Select some of the work samples you would like to include and note any design features (audio, video, etc.) that you would ideally like.

Next, look through some free e-portfolio platforms and choose one to begin.

APPLY

Create an electronic portfolio by first creating the structure. Develop a page for every major element you decided to include (Welcome Page, About Me, Resumé, Courses, Goals, Nonacademic Activities, etc.).

Then populate the Welcome and About Me pages. Next, choose one of your courses and a sample of work from it. Identify the learning outcome associated with the assignment and in a couple of paragraphs, reflect on what the assignment meant to you and why you believe it satisfies the learning outcome.

Suggested Resources

Chapter 1

Allen, E., & Seaman, J. (2010). *Learning on demand: Online education in the United States, 2009*. Newburyport, MA: The Sloan Consortium and Babson Survey Research Group.

Irizarry, R. (2002). Self-efficacy & motivation effects on online psychology student retention. *USDLA Journal, 16*(12). Retrieved May 19, 2004, from www.usdla.org/html/journal/DEC02_Issue/article07.html

National Center for Education Statistics. (2000). *Distance learning in higher education institutions* (Rep. No. NCES 2000–053). Washington, DC : National Center for Education Statistics, Office of Educational Research and Improvement, U.S. Department of Education.

Parker, A. (2003). Identifying predictors of academic persistence in distance education. *USDLA Journal, 17*(1). Retrieved March 2, 2010, from www.usdla.org/html/journal/JAN03_Issue/article06.html

U.S. Department of Education. (2009, May). *Evaluation of evidence-based practices in online learning: A meta-analysis and review of online learning studies*. Retrieved March 2, 2010, from www.geteducated.com/images/pdfs/doe_online_education_finalreport.pdf

Chapter 2

Allen, D. (2001). *Getting things done: The art of stress-free productivity*. New York: Penguin Group.

Burka, J. B., & Yuen, L. (1983). *Procrastination: Why you do it, what to do about it*. Reading, MA: Perseus Books.

Cameron, J. (1992). *The artist's way*. New York: Jeremy P. Tarcher/Putnam.

Covey, S. (1989). *Seven habits of highly effective people*. New York: Fireside/Simon & Schuster.

Ganey, L. R., Christ, F. L., & Hurt, V. R. (2005). *Online student skills and strategies handbook*. Boston: Allyn & Bacon.

Hall, E. T. (1983). *The dance of life: The other dimension of time*. Garden City, NY: Anchor Press/Doubleday.

Lambert, C. (1999). *Mind over water: Lessons on life from the art of rowing*. New York: Houghton Mifflin.

Loehr, J., & Shwartz, T. (2003). *The power of full engagement*. New York: The Free Press.

Moran, A. P. (1997). *Managing your own learning at university: A practical guide*. Dublin, Ireland: University College Press.

Parsad, B., & Lewis, L. (2008, December). *Distance education at degree-granting postsecondary institutions: 2006–07*. Retrieved February 23, 2010, from http://nces.ed.gov/pubsearch/pubsinfo.asp?pubid=2009044

Postman, Neil (2005). *Amusing ourselves to death: Public discourse in the age of television*. New York: Penguin Books.

Take charge of your time. Retrieved January 15, 2010, from http://web.mit.edu/uaap/learning/teach/time/index.html

Chapter 3

Boeree, C. G. (2006). "Carl Jung." Retrieved from http://webspace.ship.edu/cgboer/jung/html

Gardner, H. (1996). *Multiple intelligences: The theory in practice*. New York: HarperCollins.

Gardner, H. (2006). *Multiple intelligence: New horizons*. New York: Basic Books.

National Center for Learning Disabilities. (2003). "LD at a Glance." Retrieved from www.ncld.org/LDInfo Zone/InfoZone_FactSheet_LD.cfm

National Center for Learning Disabilities. "Adult Learning Disabilities: A Learning Disability Isn't Something You Outgrow. It's Something You Learn to Master" (pamphlet). New York: National Center for Learning Disabilities.

Price, D. V., & Bell, A.(2008). *Federal Access Policies and Higher Education for Working Adults*. Retrieved from www.americanprogress.org/issues/2008/10/pdf/access_policies.pdf

Chapter 4

Begley, S. (2006, October 20). Critical thinking: Part skill, part mindset and totally up to you. *Wall Street Journal*, p. B1.

Carr, R., & Ledwith, F. (2000). Helping disadvantaged students. *Teaching at a Distance, 18,* 77–85.

Carr, S. (2000, February 11). As distance education comes of age, the challenge is keeping the students. *The Chronicle of Higher Education*, pp. A39–A41.

Chyung, S. Y. (2001). Systematic and systemic approaches to reducing attrition rates in online higher education. *The American Journal of Distance Education, 15*(3), 36–49.

Lowery, L. (1998). *The biological basis of thinking and learning*. Retrieved April 2, 2004, from http://lhsfoss.org/newsletters/archive/pdfs/FOSS_BBTL.pdf

Mayer, R. E. (2001). *Multimedia learning*. New York: Cambridge University Press.

Ruggiero, V. (2001). *The art of thinking*. As quoted in "Critical Thinking," available at http://success.oregonstate.edu/criticalthinking.html

Terrell, S., & Dringus, L. (1999). An investigation of the effect of learning style on student success in an online learning environment. *Journal of Educational Technology Systems, 28*(3), 231–238.

Chapter 5

Christ, F. L., & Ganey, L. (2003). *100 things every online student ought to know.* Cambridge, England: Cambridge Stratford Publishing.

Ganey, L. R., Jr. (2001). *Becoming a successful distance learner: Eight readiness factors.* Clearwater, FL: H&H Publishing.

Madden, M., & Jones, S. (2002, September 15). *The Internet goes to college.* Pew Research Center. Retrieved August 9, 2010, from www.pewinternet.org/Reports/2002/The-Internet-Goes-to-College.aspx

Meyer, A., & Rose, D. H. Developing reading strategies. In A. Meyer & D. H. Rose, *Learning to read in the computer age.* Retrieved February 27, 2010, from www.cast.org/publications/books/ltr/chapter3.html

Rich, M. (2008, July 27). Literacy debate: Online, R U really reading? *The New York Times.* Retrieved April 22, 2010, from www.nytimes.com/2008/07/27/books/27reading.html?pagewanted=1&_r=3

Sweeney, L. (2005, August). Guidelines for being a good online student (or helping someone with learning online). *The Learning Center Newsletter.* Retrieved July 12, 2010, from www.learningassistance.com/2005/august/onlineguidelines.html

U.S. Department of Education. (2009, May). Evaluation of evidence-based practices in online learning: A meta-analysis and review of online learning studies. Retrieved March 2, 2010, from www.geteducated.com/images/pdfs/doe_online_education_finalreport.pdf

Watkins, R., & Corry, M. (2004). *E-learning companion: A student's guide to online success.* New York: Houghton Mifflin.

White, K. W., & Baker, J. D. (2004). *The student guide to successful online learning: A handbook of tips, strategies, and techniques.* Boston: Allyn & Bacon.

Chapter 6

Audesirk, T., Audesirk, G., & Byers, B. E. (2000). *Life on earth* (2nd ed.). Upper Saddle River, NJ: Prentice Hall.

Erickson, B. L., & Strommer, D. W. (1991). *Teaching college freshmen.* San Francisco: Jossey-Bass.

Gales, P. (2005). Instructor-provided notes. In B. Hoffman (Ed.), *Encyclopedia of Educational Technology.*

Jaschik, S. (2009, June 29). *The evidence on online education.* Retrieved April 22, 2010, from www.insidehighered.com/news/2009/06/29/online

Kiewra, K. A. (1985). Providing the instructor's notes: An effective addition to student note-taking. *Educational Psychologist, 20,* 33–39.

Longman, D., & Atkinson, R. (1999). *College learning and study skills.* Belmont, CA: Wadsworth/Thomson Learning.

Pauk, W. (2011). *How to study in college* (10th ed.). Boston: Houghton Mifflin.

Chapter 7

Christ, F. L., & Ganey, L. (2003). *100 things every online student ought to know.* Cambridge, England: Cambridge Stratford Publishing.

Conrad, R., & Donaldson, J. A. (2004). *Engaging the online learner: Activities and resources for creative instruction. Online teaching and learning.* San Francisco: Jossey-Bass.

Davison, Chris. (2005). *Information technology and innovation in language education.* Hong Kong: Hong Kong University Press.

Dudeney, G., & Hockly, N. (2007). *How to teach English with technology.* New York: Pearson Longman.

Everson, B. J. (1991). Vygotsky and the teaching of writing. *Quarterly of the National Writing Project and the Center for the Study of Writing and Literacy, 13*(3), 8–11.

Friedman, T. (2005). *The world is flat: A brief history of the twenty-first century.* New York: Farrar, Straus and Giroux.

Ganey, L. R., Jr. (2001). *Becoming a successful distance learner: Eight readiness factors.* Clearwater, FL: H&H Publishing.

Hanson-Smith, E., & Rilling, S. (Eds.). (2006). *Learning languages through technology.* Alexandria, VA: TESOL.

November, A. (2001). *Empowering students with technology.* Thousand Oaks, CA: Corwin Press.

Richardson, W. (2006). *Blogs, wikis, podcasts, and other powerful web tools for classrooms.* Thousand Oaks, CA: Corwin Press.

Selber, S. (2004). *Multiliteracies for a digital age.* Carbondale: Southern Illinois University Press.

Sweeney, L. (2005, August). Guidelines for being a good online student (or helping someone with learning online). *The Learning Center Newsletter.* Retrieved July 12, 2010, from www.learningassistance.com/2005/august/onlineguidelines.html

U.S. Department of Education. (2009, May). Evaluation of evidence-based practices in online learning: A meta-analysis and review of online learning studies. Retrieved March 2, 2010, from www.geteducated.com/images/pdfs/doe_online_education_finalreport.pdf

Warlick, D. (2004). *Redefining literacy for the 21st century.* Santa Barbara, CA: Linworth Publishing.

Watkins, R., & Corry, M. (2004). *E-learning companion: A student's guide to online success.* New York: Houghton Mifflin.

White, K. W., & Baker, J. D. (2004). *The student guide to successful online learning: A handbook of tips, strategies, and techniques.* Boston: Allyn & Bacon.

Chapter 8

Abrami, P., & Barrett, H. (2005). Directions for research and development on electronic portfolios. *Canadian Journal of Learning and Technology, 3.*

Lorenzo, G., & Ittelson, J. (2005). An overview of e-portfolios. *Educause Learning Initiative.* Retrieved August 9, 2010, from http://net.educause.edu/ir/library/pdf/ELI3001.pdf

Index

Index